A COUNTRY OF
STRANGERS

A COUNTRY OF STRANGERS

NEW AND SELECTED POEMS

D. Nurkse

ALFRED A. KNOPF
New York
2022

THIS IS A BORZOI BOOK
PUBLISHED BY ALFRED A. KNOPF

Copyright © 2022 by D. Nurkse

All rights reserved. Published in the United States by Alfred A. Knopf,
a division of Penguin Random House LLC, New York, and distributed
in Canada by Penguin Random House Canada Limited, Toronto.

www.aaknopf.com

Knopf, Borzoi Books, and the colophon are registered
trademarks of Penguin Random House LLC.

Select poems were first published in the following volumes: *The Rules of Paradise*
(Four Way Books, 2001) and *Leaving Xaia* (Four Way Books, 2000); *Voices Over
Water* (Graywolf, 1993); *Shadow Wars* (Hanging Loose Press, 1988); *Staggered Lights*
(Owl Creek Press, 1990); and *Isolation in Action* (State Street Press, 1988).

Library of Congress Cataloging-in-Publication Data
Names: Nurkse, D., 1949– author.
Title: A country of strangers : new and selected poems / D. Nurkse.
Description: First edition. | New York : Alfred A. Knopf, 2022. | "This is
a Borzoi book."
Identifiers: LCCN 2021028663 (print) | LCCN 2021028664 (ebook) |
ISBN 9780593321409 (hardcover) | ISBN 9780593321416 (ebook)
Subjects: LCGFT: Poetry.
Classification: LCC PS3564.U76 C68 2022 (print) | LCC PS3564.U76 (ebook) |
DDC 811/.54—dc23
LC record available at https://lccn.loc.gov/2021028663
LC ebook record available at https://lccn.loc.gov/2021028664

Jacket photograph by Matthias Clamer / Stone / Getty Images
Jacket design by Janet Hansen

Manufactured in Canada
First Edition

For Beth, with love

Contents

A Country of Strangers: New Poems

Staggered Lights

Shadow Wars

Isolation in Action

The Rules of Paradise

The Fall

Burnt Island

The Border Kingdom

Love in the Last Days

A Night in Brooklyn

A Country of Strangers: New Poems

Order to Disperse   *for the students*

Tonight my children are facing live ammunition.

One holds a rock, one brought a Bible, one hides a phone.

The fires of the provocateurs burn so brightly.

The police put duct tape over their badges.

The soldiers are hooded; they wear no insignia.

Last night they had rubber bullets, tonight hollow-point.

In the smoke you see the outlines of a bank, a cathedral,

absent as the profiles of Presidents on coins.

A voice advances, a voice retreats, someone aims.

Have you ever died in a dream? What happened then?

Tell me what happened! There is only one life.

How long will I hold mine like water in cupped hands?

The Detentions

In death too there are great cities, streets of padlocked binderies under rain that tastes of piss, cathedrals with bricked-in windows, garages lit by droplights, tenements with narrow stairs covered by linoleum treads worn smooth as the ball of a thumb. Catch your breath on any landing: a heart or a name will be scratched into the wall.

Here too is the dim room where lovers test each other, as you push against the slats of a fence, word after word, caress after caress. Here too you hear cars whoosh in the distance, crazily absent, and lights cross the ceiling, as if a child flung a handful of rice. A scrap of passing music calls you, more intimate than a voice.

Here too a red glare pulses and someone shouts. Again you look down from a great height. Is the man in cuffs drunk? Why is he staggering? Again you have to decide: do I yell out the window and show where I live? Do I take a video on my cell? Where would I send it? Do I run down those endless flights, into the street, waving my hands and commanding *no*? Would I at least be able to memorize the license plate? Would it be blank?

Even at the end of death. Prepare yourself. Even where there is no I. No judgment, no reward.

Only the long street, the gray rain, the boarded shops, a few passersby, their eyes kept down, the lamps shining inward.

In the City of Statues

When we were old and knew
we would never see Canaan
we woke in the same breath
dressed shivering, gulped instant,
and trudged to the rally point
with our Magic Marker pasteboard
to chant ourselves speechless
though we did not believe the slogans
and the crowd was all strangers—
(once we saw a child who looked
like you forty years ago and once
young lovers with our own grievance
and resolve)—facing us, batons,
gas canisters, hoses, stun guns,
grenades, and the strange machine
that can decipher the human face.

In the Winter of Painted Swastikas

The demonstration is winding down,
the sound system has been dismantled
and stashed in numbered boxes,
students draped in frayed banners
are flirting or commiserating,
there's still a sense of safety
lingering though the streets
home are icy, dark, and watched,
and if two women hold hands
a helmet on a rooftop will shout
girls coming from the march.

The Polls

What if asthma strikes
in the line outside Medgar Evers?
Supposing your sugar drops
and you sway—the next person
can't catch you: *distance*.

Dawn is so far away
you can't see your right hand
yet the crowd fires its own neurons—
advance six steps, shuffle, pause—
as if you were deep in a body
whose mind finally knows itself

and the Methodist sirens are faint now.
Give it another hour, five minutes,
one Mississippi . . . no one leaves.
Now a conversation has kindled
and there is no hatred in these voices

murmuring through masks:
Miss Geraldine Baxter gone
to Redeemer, Iris Sanchez lost
in Mercy, and no way to mourn
except: hold on one more breath.

The Screen

I invited my mother to visit and watch. A woman being elected President! We sat in front of cable news. I swear we each thought of holding hands. After twenty minutes, we began to fidget. She excused herself to the bathroom. I chose to take a call. I buried my eyes in my cell.

Our city had grown so silent. Where were the ambulances, the low-flying jets? A car passed with the rattle of a loose fan belt. A child cried in the next building. I have to go, my mother said suddenly, home to feed my Maltese.

I helped her into her coat and found her gloves. We hugged a little stiffly. I heard her steps diminish in the corridor. I was left facing the screen. I tore myself away and followed her—she is old, old! I rode the next elevator down.

Were our streets ever so dark? The lamps were shining with a prissy glow that disclosed nothing, that smudged whatever it touched. But I saw a silhouette with her adamant shuffle and followed it into the cold.

I watched from a block away as she hailed a cab, clambered in gimpily, lit a cigarette and began chatting. The car sped away toward Queens. So it is long ago, I thought, she can smoke and flirt. Perhaps I am not even born yet.

And I began walking, endlessly, in our vast city. Doors flew open and the faces there were the children who died in Birmingham, in Lowndes County and Neshoba. But the high windows were blank and pulsed with a shuddering blue light.

Marbles and a Dead Bee

1
Imago was elected this morning—
in the gray hour before dawn
the last firewall crumbled.
A street drunk moans
in ecstasy or shame.

2
Close your eyes. Imago controls
the House, Senate, Supreme Court.
Open them. Just sunlight on a blind.

3
As a dropped lightbulb shatters
so my country.

4
The poet will defend herself with poetry,
the lover with sex,
the child with marbles and a dead bee,
the suicide with suicide.

5
But if you choose to kill yourself
find a quiet room in the past.

Tonight your life is required for a task.

Caligula

After Suetonius

Caligula ordered the night city illuminated.
Every stoop, porch, or balcony was a stage.

He made the senators dress as prostitutes—
tight silk skirts, paste-on eyelashes.
Up to a matron to wriggle into a boy's shorts.

Marcus Severus, one-armed veteran
of our labyrinthine border wars,
had to hobble into the amphitheater
armed with a plume, and attack a lion.

A plume! We were fascinated.
We were all players, who was the audience?

The Emperor chose *me, me, me,* and *me,*
and slept with us. He was passive
as a bedpost, but listed his demands
in documents we had to sign in advance.

Slaves—who had been stockbrokers
or insurance agents a moment ago—
carried triremes on their backs to Rome.
Sails billowed above our seven sacred hills.

Would it ever end? We were enthralled.
Every breath was a saga
when you long to skip to the finale.

We no longer washed, brushed our teeth,
or picked a scab—just *him, him, him.*

It was Cassius Chaerea who killed him—
that silent tribune he called "pansy."

The Emperor lay on his golden bed.
We were mesmerized. All we could do
was compete to reconstruct the portents:
headless chicken racing all morning,
kitten born without eyes, huge cloud,
tiny cloud, cloud like a fist . . .

For a few hours the Chronicler
listened and scribbled, but soon
he grew bored, we bored ourselves,
so began Caligula's slow death—

Caligula who so often said of a captive,
"make him feel he's really dying."

Now we're helpless as always,
faced with twilight, a child crying,
birdsong, the breeze, our seven steep hills.

The White Prisons

The kids ask: *do you also teach in the white prisons?*

There are white schools, white libraries, white hospitals, churches, parks and ball fields, why wouldn't there be white prisons?

Snow pulses in a tiny barred window: an idea at once vague and obsessive.

The kids have been writing their poem. It starts with the blank page, a doodle in the margin, but soon you are a child in the streets. Oily slush seeps up through the soles of your Nikes. You pass a Burger King, Zion Redeemer, the ironworks under sleet. Pitkin Avenue does not go all the way to morning. The white Lexus appears out of nowhere. Where to run: icy stoops, steel-shod doors.

I expect to live another three years. Maybe two and six weeks. Six weeks and seven days. Probably to my nineteenth birthday.

It happens every night in my mind. The long street, the hour before dawn, the white Lexus, my enemy's face in the tinted window. So familiar. So masked.

Conversation Behind the White Curtain

I will protect myself and my family.

I will bury ninety gallons of fresh water,
stash rice and beans in steel boxes,
hide a bike with freshly oiled gears
to glide between the rows of stuck cars

says one voice.

I will keep a gun with a single bullet

says a second voice.

I foresaw this all my life but when it came
I could not recognize it—it had the face
of wind and rain, the shining face of days.

I want to go back to who I was,
the house with a beehive in the pines,
the brook breaking all night over stones.

Let me go back to the child swinging,
the dog digging, the cat hiding under the car,
the cloud of moths—take me back! Accept me.

The ants help each other—they carry fat crumbs,
bury their dead and sweep their narrow paths.
The wasps can recognize each other's faces,
you and you, in the chaos of the swarm.
The bees dance a language: here is nectar.

I want to go back to being a body. A voice with eyes.

So we say. But we all speak at once.

The Arrow Creek Fire

I'm playing hide-and-seek with the child. In my dark spot behind the sofa, I turn on my cell and scroll to the news.

The child is still counting. *Eleven, three, six minus, twelve times . . .* some numbers she copies off Middle Sister, some she never knew or has forgotten since the beginning of summer, some she worships and doesn't dare speak out loud. At least one she hates so bitterly she stammers to utter it. On my screen the Arrow Creek Fire appears, like a flower blooming in time-lapse photography. The names of the dead begin to cross the picture, quickly, quickly, as if hurrying to school or work.

With half a mind, I listen to the child poking behind the piano, opening closet doors, laughing to herself, becoming impressed, then annoyed, calling me as you might call a dog, then as you might summon a cat. The plume is fifty-five thousand feet tall and tornadic. Shot through with dry lightning, it generates its own pressure system, its own agency.

Now the rattle of the kitchen drawers opening. I could not possibly be there. My Samsung phone is hot in my palm. Will it shut itself down automatically? I am watching with such hunger. The child must be tired. Is she fixing herself a peanut butter sandwich? I can smell the crisp almost bitter crust being cut away, the fluffy Nature's Way bread, the sweet remains on the knife blade.

I am here. Look for me. It's a million and one *now*!

Or will you find just the empty space? The template of the body in dust? A bee lying on its back piously, feelers up? Did I live long ago? Was I absent then as I am now?

Showers

The child tells me, *put a brick in the toilet,*
don't wear leather, don't eat brisket,
snapper, or farmed salmon—not tells,
orders—doesn't she know the sluice gates
were left open and a trillion gallons
wasted just for the dare of it?

Until the staring eye shares that thrill,
confessing: *I am just iris and cornea,*
blind spot where brain meets mind,
the place where the image forms itself
from a spark—*image of the coming storm.*

But the child waits outside the bathroom
with the watch she got for Best Diorama
muttering, *two minutes too long.*

Half measures, I say. She says, *action*.
I: *I'm one man.* She: *Seven billion.*

If you choose, the sea goes back.

The Commands

The child taught the dog *stay*
by staying herself, in the dark garden,
and the dog imitated her.

The child taught the dog *fetch*
by pushing a twig with her nose.

She taught the dog *come*
by appearing out of the pines
(there were only two pines
and she had to bribe the dog
with a biscuit not to follow her).

She taught the dog *heel*.
Always there had been a gap
like a missing tooth, just out of reach,
and now apparently it was the dog
with his ropy ears, quirky itches,
and faintly hopeless grin.

She taught *adore me* and *don't die*.
The dog listened, head cocked,
but his square nose swiveled
to watch a firefly stitching
in and out of leaf shadow.

Immediately it was twilight
and a voice called *dinner*.

The child taught *voice*
and *you must obey*.
By now the dog was bored
and trotted away, perhaps hoping
to dig up a dead vole

out of the system of tunnels
that undermined those dusty peonies.

The child panted after,
shouting all the lessons at once,
adore me, stay, dinner, come,
heel, fetch, don't die
so they sounded savage
like a sob or the name of God
until the dog was scared
and bounded across Glenwood
into the neighbor's yard
or the neighbor's neighbor's,
and the voice (which was mine)
spluttered *now, this minute, at once*—

at once other voices were shouting
you must, you can't, never, always,
no, come back, with an edge of panic
or triumph or unbearable weariness—

but it was night and the firefly
vanished into its own burning planet.

The Body

1

A small animal, perhaps an otter,
darted under our wheels.
My wife was driving.
No time to swerve.
I sensed no impact.
She braked. I scrutinized
the tarmac for blood.

Nothing, not a scrap of fur,
though the road seemed to hum,
alert as skin to the touch.

Reek of pepper and must.
Pent-up hush of late summer.

Behind a scrim of willows,
a glint seemed to slip backwards.

2

Before we were born
we found ways not to exist,
happily, playfully.
thriving on no-fish
a billion billion years
before the universe exploded.

No one missed us,
we didn't miss ourselves.
There was no absence.

3

Leery of ticks,
we part ash leaves
and here's Gihon River,

an ant clinging stoically
to a frayed petal, a bee
flying gamely underwater.

4
Evening. We won't come back
to this angle of scorched tar,
logged forest choked with brush,
Canada hunched behind a bluff.

A farmhouse lights as we watch—
porch, then kitchen, like a toy.

You can hear a child intoning
the score of a jump rope game
solemnly, with sleepy urgency,
as if blurting out a secret,
every syllable held and slurred
in the loud shush of current.

Radio signals link galaxies
but we're so close
all we know of ourselves
is the blur of an eyelash.

After us, the white line, the wall of pines.

Marriage in the Mountains

After a wedding with no witness
she brought me home to Sandgate,
star moss and acorn lids.

A skeeter flung its V
across puddle glint
but she straddled it
with her long fastidious step.

A farm dog padded up
but she motioned it back
to its too-red barn
with a calm adamant nod.

It was early in a foggy spring.

I was married to a murmur,
a shrug, a quarter-turn,
an exhale, a pirouette—

pledged to a bead of dew
flashing in a cobweb,
to the luminous faintly hairy
inner side of a beech leaf.

Only a few more summers
in her high country
of terraced copses,
lime kilns, knots of hardwood.

I belonged in the world
like a pinecone or passing cloud.

Ischia

That city was a game we played against each other
with a mirror, a dusty bottle of Prosecco,
various empty shoes of different sizes,
a sliver of Mediterranean in an incised window.
The object was to lose, ignominiously,
and we allowed ourselves extraneous elements:
the fly; an extremely faint marching band
celebrating independence in a distant plaza;
nakedness, a mole, paradise, suffering, time.
We would begin at twilight and end at sunrise.
To the loser, Ischia would be a memory,
to the winner, a conquest to be administered.
If it was a draw, we would just listen
arm in arm to the great bells ringing,
booming, thrumming, the ropes creaking,
triumphant and still powerless
before the inhuman weakness of dawn.

Early Morning, Late Summer, Unmade Bed

Remember the suffering of this pronoun *I*,
how this vowel was slighted and betrayed,
how this letter undressed and lay awake
until dawn, when even the logy oaks
were overburdened with the Self,
even the mirror, window, wineglass

were inhabited by a glint, a radiant edge.
Then she knelt at the head of the bed
to unzip her boot, fork and spoon were reconciled,
this letter was lost in a heaven that hurt
like the labyrinthine labor of the racing mind.
Take your sharp pencil, love, and erase me
from the top down, leaving a smudge
to darken between the naked sleepers.

Money

Once I made her take all the items
out of the grocery bag and tick them off
against the receipt while the old dog
watched through a sheen of cataracts.

What is this item, I asked, CSPK?
She showed me: it was the root
of a fruit I had never tasted,
sweet and salty. It was my death
that I once knew by heart and now
try to mollify by counting.
It was dark night coming
when we doze side by side
in separate dreams of marriage.

And there were other issues.
Why three cans of stewed pears
when they were offered at nine for twelve?

The cat commented:
"I was going to the garden
to kill a fat rabbit but
you can't afford a sparrow,
only a blue moth so weightless
it drifts against the open claw."

I knew it was a code but I
was the Husband, seven letters
of an alphabet, one of the chess pieces
that must find a way to move the hand—
exploit the arrogance of the right,
the diffidence of the left—

Let the sparrow, eloquent in death,
teach me from the cat's mouth
how to live in time.

This Life

After swimming in Kiln Lake we were so tired,
you and I, we dried ourselves with the nubby towel
that smells of dog, then slept side by side
in the tall grass, careless of ticks—when we woke
it was this life, we dried each other again
with our fingertips, Venus had risen, and a red star
flashing at the horizon, Antares or Betelgeuse:
as always we waited for a sign, let this life
be a sign: we heard the frogs calling, almost ranting,
and saw no one, the rushes bent to our shape,
a glowworm, two clumps of breathing earth.

Game with a Mad Bounce

The child and I are kicking
a pebble down the road—

the child is Gautama
the pebble is Saint Teresa
and I'm no one: or

we are both Gramsci
the road is Maimonides
and you are no one: or

the child counts steps to Frogurt
I'm an old man with cancer
the pebble is no one and

no one loves us so

it's raining in the White Mountains

but here just the pang of wood smoke—

here joy and sorrow
are a fence and a lit window—

here God's silence
is the silence of a cricket.

Flora of the Boreal Forest

The child insisted on being carried
to touch the pine, the oak, oak, pine,
and I grew numb under that adamant voice.
My arm throbbed as she tried to decide:
Cone? Acorn? Needle? Leaf?

It's only thanks to the half-light
that we can go home, she prancing
on my shoulder, trying to braid
my wisp of hair, singing absently.

Thrush or vireo, loud and invisible,
slurring two maniac notes:
wherever it calls from is the center.

Lake behind the scrim of alder
like a plenitude you long for
all your life, most of all at the end.

Lit window like a force
you can't imagine knowing you
but it consumes you without reflection.

World like a hole to fall into
forever, or else a curtain
you might stick your hand through.

Soon even she will tire of her song,
how it meets itself coming and going,
the vast spaces between notes,
the snarky refrain, Damariscotta,
the first faint stars, and she'll put
her sticky hand over my eyes: pine.

Evening in the Pines

The dog barking across the lake,
the guitar that thinks it's human,
the cricket practicing to be a cricket,
the thrush puffed up with attitude—

all to impress a listener
but there is no listener.

August and a spindled leaf,
a blue moth sailing backwards,
the pigtail girls on the island
pouring make-believe tea
into cups too delicate to see—

all to make a watcher cry
but there is no watcher.

Human mind, created by birdsong,
night sky and a dollop of rain,
why do you cling so fiercely
to the aftertaste of burnt sugar?

Turn and face yourself
if there is a self.

A Clearing on Ruth Island

The child sees the firefly far off in the birches. It's very late. I did not expect another summer, another child, so much darkness. She trots away to catch it. Possibly nine minutes later, she lopes back, barely winded. There is the light in her cupped hands. She shows it off: look how it flashes. She will pass it to me. I can feel the little wind and the adamant wing against my palms. My life is almost over. I pass it back. She waves it up dramatically. We watch for a greenish spark. If the night is clear and we can stare up for a full minute, we are guaranteed to see a satellite, a star whose name I know—there are only five—a glittering meteor, a comet, or the glint of a plane headed to the Arctic.

Those towering ghostly shapes must be the huge unmoving cumulus of late summer, the clouds Jesus referred to when he said "in my father's house there are many mansions." These close low humpbacked shapes must be the fishermen's boats, hauled high and tarped.

No lamps on the island. What light there is seems to come from under our sneakers. Now the fireflies are pulsing in phase—you could parse it out, like the meter of a fugue.

The plan is obvious. Earth will become more and more beautiful until I can't stand it. Then I will vanish. It will be in my mind that the skiffs are hauled up, safe from the wild tide. In my mind that the silly sleepless accordion plays "Sweet Loraine," oversweet across deep water.

I can't see the child but she takes my pinkie, almost angrily. She will lead me back to Scoffield, counting our steps on the dark path. When we come to a million, we will be home.

The Unendurable Tests

Here is my doctor on the pebbled path
talking on his cell to someone he loves
desperately, who just left for Canada.

I hear awe in his voice, rage, bereavement,
wild laughter; he gestures with his free hand,
casting shadow arabesques—now a note
of abject submission as he bargains—
he has nothing to bargain with—

meanwhile I'm scrunched behind a potted palm
in an alcove of Pulmonary Court waiting
for a lull so I can saunter out
casually and ask: *did I pass?*

Here in a darkness no bigger than the body
six wasps are curled, feelers in the air.
Here's a spindled Bazooka wrapper,
the cogwheel from a smashed watch,

and someone has carved a heart
and a date in the brick itself: today.

The Fire

War is a breath away but my neighbors can't believe it.

I ring their doorbells and tell them: maybe not this May, but next June
at the latest. They stare straight past me, at the maze of tiny lawns, the
sprinklers, a kid on a bike hurling the Globe onto stoops.

An old man invites me in and offers me macaroons. You look tense, he
says. The armies, I recite, are facing each other in the Middle East. But
it just reminds him of his childhood, which is mine. Didn't I push him
off the high swing?

Now his mind has wandered, he begins nibbling the macaroon he
offered me, all along the edges, revolving it in his hands rapidly, like a
squirrel.

The bombing, I say, happens at the speed of light. Once it starts it can't
stop. I trot out statistics. Surely the seventh zero will touch him?

But he is sweeping the crumbs into the palm of his left hand, coaxing
them, counting them, perhaps naming them under his breath, like
Adam. His lips are moist.

And how to leave him? He is shockingly frail, wasted even. When
I describe the effects of radiation, he gazes past me out the open
door, blinking. Sundown in the maples. A child with a Frisbee. A
Newfoundland squatting on its haunches, calculating expertly when the
high glide will bank and veer.

The fire, I say, and the old man nods. He has miniature pecan pies, and
he unwraps their many layers of foil. It will take at least fifteen minutes
for them to thaw. Can we get to the point, he says indulgently.

But now I am just arguing—my voice is so thick and furry it irks me, like
a trapped ferret in my throat—that it will rain all tomorrow. All the long
night. Gray dawn and the first hours of morning.

A Lullaby

I rocked the child
in the crook of my arm
and mouthed "Goodnight Irene"
until her moth-wing eyelids
twitched, the sobbing stopped,
she seemed bewildered
not to wail, breath came easy.
I set her down softly.
on her mother's quilt.

Then I felt the loneliness
of a planet falling
into nothing, nothing, nothing.

The Chime

When death stands in your doorway, you must show no weakness. If he points at his watch, answer "in five minutes." If he insists, murmur "just a minute." When he bridles, whisper "half a minute," "a second," "half a sec," "one moment."

You mustn't look him in the eye. But don't avert your gaze. Glance decisively at the bridge of the nose or the moist place right below the lips.

If he unfolds a map, please don't express a preference for the seashore or the mountains. Betray no longing or anxiety. You might tap the margin nonchalantly, if there is a margin.

There's an old superstition that death is a healer, he brings peace, escape from corruption. On the contrary: he is not a person, an animal, an insect, not even a pebble. Not even a name. Not an event. Not a whiff of night air.

So why, ask yourself, does he fidget there, with that peevish "can't we meet each other halfway" expression, in those absurd Goodwill clothes, baggy corduroy suit, pants and jacket the same color but different wales, so often folded the seams are white as chalk lines, fat two-tone white-and-beige golf shoes with cleats, nylon argyle socks, like someone's idea of an encyclopedia salesman from the nineteen thirties?

And why is the street behind him so fascinating, empty as a stage set, a few vans double-parked, a cat hiding under one, sometimes the flicker of the tip of a tail, sometimes the glint of the eye itself, voracious, ecstatic?

A Country of Strangers

1

"It was a place I never heard of," a woman said, "though I studied geopolitics in college and worked as a secretary for an embassy. I Googled it. No hits. Nothing in the card catalog. Yet I kept overhearing that name, outside a clinic or in a church basement. A voice would say, 'I have family there. There was a coup. The suffering is indescribable. The famine. The corruption. Useless to send help. My cousin never writes.'"

The speaker was my age, a vein pulsing on her temple, proud in her carriage. She addressed a friend who seemed completely uninterested, absently checking her messages.

I was just an eavesdropper, heading north myself, in the crowd outside the departure platform. I wanted to interrupt, "that nation is Sheol, the limousines and shanties, padlocked granaries and empty fields, live wires strung in the rain. Of course no relative returns."

But our line was starting to move. Sleepily the travelers gathered their suitcases tied with twine, their sacks made of canvas sewn shut, their boxes—some contained animals whose eyes you saw glinting, whose pulse you sensed, though they were silent, patently willing themselves to be silent. A boy trundled a live fish in a cellophane bag of water. It darted like a flame. He kept the top sealed with his right thumb and forefinger, his left hand was cupped, supporting the weight. He held his ticket in his teeth. A little girl in a grimy lace dress brandished a cricket in a matchbox. She shook it to make it sing, and held it to her ear. It sang regardless, coldly, imperious. The man behind her, whose chalky face was wrinkled like a pug's, had hoisted himself upright. Now he nudged her forward with the rubber tip of his cane.

2

Understand that our country is poor too, here too the lamps flicker, here too a toothache is incurable. Here too every inch of the border is sealed.

Not Yet America

At the end we are marching and yelling, waving signs we inked in ourselves, just as we did when we were kids.

The street never changes. Drinkers watch from a bar, suds glinting on their upper lips. A bald man is being shaved in a barbershop. The chair swivels toward us: how round those eyes are, in a face smothered under lather. A baker in a white paper bag hat stares from a doorway, poised to clap flour from his hands. Behind an iron grille, a nun sighs and crosses herself.

Apparently we will always have to march, singing to keep awake, calling "peace" and "justice" as if those sibilants could answer: in the numbing cold, even in the night sky, in the empty quadrant of Scorpio.

There you'll find us, and the street too, since it stretches forever. A bodega with steel gates. A Jiffy Lube. A chain-link fence on which a child has spray-painted the first stroke of the first letter of a name.

Staggered Lights

Small Countries

A man and a woman
are lying together
listening to news of a war.
The radio dial
is the only light in the room.
Casualties are read out.
He thinks, "Those are people
I no longer have to love,"
and he touches her hair
and calls her name
but it sounds strange to her
like a stone left over
from a house already built.

Grandmother's Exile

The birds sang in a dead tree.
All summer, she'd heard the axe
in the pines, and branches collapsing
as if a bear were escaping
inland. At night all she heard
was the cistern leak
until it froze in a string
and each drop was a pearl.
Then the wind came from Lapland.
She lost the hand to frostbite.
She called the ache in the phantom limb
"America," and when the sea calmed
she crossed it: the rest of her life
is accounted for, entered in code
in the blank front page of a King James Bible.

The Settlement

1945: the batters
are swinging for the fences.
The wind drives all flies foul.
In a small town in Canada
my grandfather watches in disbelief:
he does not know
what the diagonal path
means for him, or what the wheat
stretching beyond the bleachers
to the Arctic means for his children.
In the ninth a ball lands fair:
the crowd shouts Ah; he whispers Ah.
At dusk a crystal radio
brings news of peace
in the Pacific Theater.
That night he dreams of the old country,
the storm bending the pines,
turning the lakes a color
blank as the name of God.
When he wakes he hunts
for that north wind and finds it
singing in the wire of his new enormous fence.

Time

In a dream I came to a city of porches
supported by wooden pillars, one sawn
a few inches off the ground.

I found a street of shuttered houses:
some of the windows were trompe l'oeil,
painted in perspective on limestone walls.
and one house was for sale.

I walked into a tearoom and there I met
my mother who has been dead three years.
Instantly I said "I know you're really dead,"
and the trance remained between us like a glass
                                        partition
—we each came to one side and didn't try to break it,
afraid of being engulfed
in the wind from nowhere.

                         *

My mother had brought a companion,
an elderly lady, who complimented her
on the way her jacket matched her bag
and the curl in her hair, asking
"how do you keep yourself
so pulled together?": my mother answered
instantly, a little bitterly
but also triumphantly, "Time."

And her friend, understanding
the will can use the pressure of days
to create form where there is none,
smiled and nodded and began
cutting a honeycake in ever smaller pieces.

Starting Again in the Orchard Country

"The new age is born,
the old rolls on unfinished."
The socks almost darned. The beam
trimmed, but as yet no roof.
In August heat we hate each other
and sleep together sopping.
A stranger comes at night
and stands in the garden
and sings in every unknown language.
In starlight his face is like my father's,
in lamplight like my mother's.
He opens his hands
to show he brought no weapon
though he comes from the land of sticks and stones.

The Windfall Mountains

One orchard is separated from the next
by fences humming with faint current.
We pry slack wire open
with a fallen branch, squeeze through,
keep hiking toward the coast.
At twilight we find a shack
full of old ladders, and we make love
until we've lost all our credentials
in suffering, and we make love again
and give up all the authority
of being lost. Sometimes in the dark
we dream the cider company's hidden cameras
are recording us, but when we wake
drifting blossoms have covered our trail.

Order

Last night I worked for an old artisan.
He sent me to his basement shop
with a weak flashlight, to mix concrete.
The tools and ruler on his pegboard
cast huge shadows, that did not
flinch when I snapped his droplight on:
only my body had no shadow.

Looking closer I saw
he was a maniac for order and had painted
the ideal forms of Hammer and Saw
in tar behind each appointed hook.

This is how I've lived
since I've known you: the tools
scatter, their shadows
stay put, to be polished,
to cut if necessary.

Paradise

One thread of paradise
is woven in her dress.
But only one. I turn over
the fabric while she's gone.
And I've lived all my life
learning how to endure pain,
how to sit in cheap hotels
and not ask, and be
empty like the bottle,
naked like the chair, narrow
like the crack in the thin cold wall.

The Engagement in the Plains

Suddenly she didn't know me
the way the fence post, the passing cars
and the silent owl don't know me:
this was some miracle of forgetting
forged in a narrow bed
in the empty part of summer
before dawn, when the clock stopped,
in the wheat country.

I looked up a word she'd whispered to me
and the page had been ripped from the dictionary.
I pored over the album
showing her as a little girl
at play with her sisters
—her eyes had been erased.

Only a note taped to the mirror
invited me to meet her
in a bar in the market town
ruled by the evangelists.

I sat on my revolving stool
while dimpling churchwomen
in bridesmaids' gowns
passed into a locked back room.
Then I heard sighs, and glass shattering.

The goldfish in a tiny bowl
stared at me
as if astonished at my drunkenness.
Staring back I understood
I'd grown old and my body
had become a trap.

Beyond it stretched the world of bitter work,
the stubble fields where the combine
gathers up the winter wheat.

Repairs

Waking, I see the tracks.

I drove here after midnight
past garages lit like gauge numbers
and a brickworks boarded up with plywood.
Behind the Traveler's Lodge I saw
a region of sky crisscrossed with wires,
the hook of a crane above a floodlit wall.

It's a repair yard
below my room,
a shunting field.

A caboose from Duluth, blue chicory
pale with first light under the wheels.
A boxcar without doors
stuffed with black oranges.

I know each morning I wake here
the fog from the Ohio will lift a little,
I'll see more scattered hammers,
more ties, an older caboose.

At night I'll pretend I'm intimate
with what we were: a small shadow
tame under the light switch, a teacup
full of the local white wildflowers
called Nobody's Fault, the switch signal
unflinching in chintz curtains.

In sleep my presentiment
will race ahead with a red fanlight,
while I trudge behind
and the steel parallels
converge on a fixed point
that exists only in the past.

Barrier Islands

The tide passed over us.
Then we slept as before
but tasting in each other furrows
and forests of distance deeply rooted.

We lived in hotels paid by the hour
after the end of vacation.
The windows glittered one by one
so long as there was writing
in Arabic, on the sea's face.

In the drawer and bed we found shells,
their spark of warning now disbelief;
whatever lived there had retreated
to an emptiness larger than the air.

Walking on the Highway

Curving shoulder
freeway above Burlington
lights of a minor city, and North
by Canada no lights. Good luck
is holy and bad luck the last town
with its rabbit coops and one boutique.
I've been traveling five years.
I still come to places seen in dreams
but not often. Lamps of a sawmill
and a maple sugar shop. Almost dawn.
No traffic. Stars
high and oblique. By my fruits
I am known.

Lamps and Fences

When the dead came into power
at first we did not notice

the stars were a little brighter
there were more roaches
wherever we walked
we killed something

since it was involuntary
it happened as if in secret

in the bars the prices
were written in chalk

the musicians were too eager to finish
though they remained true
to the old rage

When we made love
our thoughts turned to the hunted

and those turned back
from the frontier

though the frontier was only
the meaning of a sound
in a language that had mastered us.

Shadow Wars

The Physical

The man beside me in the line
in the Draft Board lobby
told me he'd just fasted nine days.
He said once before he'd fasted eighteen
just to clear the mucus from his system
and once for twelve to dominate his passions,
but this was the first time
the visions he saw were Satanic:
as he tried to describe them his face
began to tic and he composed himself
so he would not seem like us common frauds:
he combed his hair in front of the see-thru mirror
and breathed deep, and recalled that the quota
was almost zero, the war had shifted to the air.

Spring Formal

After the dance
we sauntered home
hand in hand.
We chose the street
our parents had forbidden
because it was too poor.
Halfway down, the engines
muscled past us:
by the time we came
to the end of the block
firemen were fumbling
at their wall of tight-rolled hoses
and we stood arm in arm
while the people who lived there
gathered around us
in bathrobes or pajamas
watching without comment
as the stone began to crack.
A river of sparks
flowed straight up,
a fireman entered
a blank window: for a moment
we could see clear
through the shell to the lights
of the next street.
Then the wall of smoke rose.
We ran on
pretending not to hurry
and kissed in her yard,
and I walked home alone
in dawn cold treasuring
the sting where her tongue
had entered my mouth
for a split second, and sniffing
the smoke on the cuff of my rented tux.

Resistance

for Elmer Maas and the Plowshares Eight

The door bangs
a key turns
and you're left alone,
your conscience almost appeased
but with the same impending death
as when you were indifferent.
Nothing in the cell
except the cold power
that your enemies, the bored
judges, clerks, doctors,
have promised will turn on you
and drive you into empty heaven.
What you remember is the witnesses:
the van driver, the stenographer,
the defendants in petty cases,
plus the imploring eyes
of a dozen of your supporters
chanting in the rain
with placards of your name,
each obscuring the next:
and now instead of consequence,
keys jangle above and below
and radios blare
a dozen different pounding love songs
deeper and deeper inside the prison.

The Roof of the Handbag Factory

We made love under the water tank
and even where our bodies
ebbed and lapped, there were still
bits of handbags: buckle tongues,
rosewood grips, doeskin swatches.
We sensed the polishing wheel
thrumming a story beneath us.
The foreman screamed our names.
After an hour, a bee landed on us, walked
where our bellies met, and flew off.
Then we tasted the silence at the heart
of a huge city in midsummer: at dusk
even the machines snapped off
and we were alone, hungry,
enraged at each other, feeling cheated,
having exchanged our infinite futures
—a raise every eighteen months—
for the rickety train to a single room.

A Vagrant

The sun setting in my eyes
darkened the traffic lights.
We were leaving the capital.
At the intersection of 100th Avenue
I watched from the corner of my eye
as three officers searched a drifter.
They ran their fingers through his hatband
and pinched his shoes: one stroked
a gun, one stared into evening,
indifferent, perhaps embarrassed,
a third barked orders in slow motion
as if the traveler and the watchers
and the street and the world itself
were all time frozen solid.
A car honked behind me and I realized
the lights had clicked several times.
Dusk had gone and my lights
were still out and she beside me
had smoked her cigarette to the quick.
I floored the pedal in a surge
of dime store lights, saying nothing,
and we were quiet in the mountains, each
feeling we'd betrayed the other
from the start, and could relax
like an old married couple.

G.E. Nonviolent Action

We shuffle in that line
of nuns and disabled veterans.
Our candles keep going out.
Chants flare and die.
We can joke under our breath
but when we come to the production gate
we're locked into righteous silence
while the remote engineers
in tinted glasses walk
the few dangerous steps
from their named parking spots
to the steel-shod glass doors.
The cameras focus automatically
and caress our images
in their vacant memory.
Our speaker says
Pray for those who make weapons,
and we bow our heads, and the voice adds
Pray for those who pay for weapons
and we pray for ourselves.
Our fingers fumble with buttons
as the wind leans from the border.
The old murmur in Latin.
In the shadow of watchtowers
that look abandoned, that block
the only road out of town,
we take refuge in our weakness
as if we possessed the hideous power
of all the choices not made.
The vigil is over
and the die-in begins.
One of us crosses a line
and throws blood, and howls
while the rest flinch
at such bad acting, and then follow,

writhing in the parking lot,
glancing up at the clouds
that glide, massive as states, north.
The engineers are long gone.
The police appear from nowhere,
from camouflaged buses, in the uniforms
of four counties, and this time
they are ruthlessly polite,
calling the spattered bodies Sir and Ma'am,
reminding us of our rights, determined
to ease the nuns into the vans,
yearning to release us
on our own recognizance
or in the custody of any name
left vacant in the dying world.

The Turn

Two cops in uniform
in an unmarked car
with a sticker reading
Rock Capital of Western NY
pull me to the curb.
One stands with his hand on his gun,
his whole body pulled askew
by the weight of the trigger.
The other explains in a mild voice
that I signaled a left turn
and proceeded straight
nine blocks back on Maple.
They ask politely that I wait
for the computer check.
They take all identification.
I sit in my car, they sit in theirs,
their fender at my door,
high beams at my nape . . .
I imagine the names of empty winter states
Dakota Nevada flashing on a screen
or perhaps the files are all in code
and I catch myself saying my name
to myself again and again
as my love said it an hour ago,
my voice rising to her pitch
first in frenzy and at last
in a gasp of disbelief.

The Unborn

She lived with him for seven years
but he didn't want a child.
She asked her married friends, why not,
why not, but they were in a different world,
sleepless: to them the question
led only to the past. She took her calendars
for the seven years and shoved them
in the incinerator. She began to shout at him
do the dishes, oil the lock,
and he put on the white apron
or the blue denim and obeyed her,
losing himself, like salt in water,
in the silence of his task.

The Second Stroke

A friend from work
comes to tell you
your mother had another problem,
and he was notified
because you once left
his number on a form.
He offers to drive you
to the emergency ward.
In the sooty rain you sense
the weight of his concentration
on the road and the power
of his concern for you,
a virtual stranger: in the corridor
he opens doors without your knowing it,
signs names, enters the ward first,
leads you to her bed
and when she sees him
she shakes her head: No
and when she sees you
she shakes her head: No.

The Visitors

After your mother dies
you linger in the waiting room
with the other families.
You ask the parents of the scalded child
how their little one is, and they answer
the graft has taken. But the old woman
says her husband still cannot speak
and only follows her with his eyes.
When you're asked about your mother
you say she died. Then they come to you
and touch you very lightly
on the sleeve of your coat
and look at you with bright eyes
and there's silence. At last someone opens
another in that stack of old magazines
and you understand it's time to go,
you must now shake hands with the surgeon
who understands everything about death.

The Ancient War

I rode beside her
on the bus to the capital.
I bragged of all the rallies
I'd been to since childhood,
all the arrests and gassings
and only a few were lies.
Factories slipped by
and the groomed highway forest
and then we were motionless
in the shadow of monuments
and the crowd formed, and I lost her.
I marched all day
thinking I was hearing her voice
in the slogans that echoed
from the empty crypts: at dusk
I met her by the chartered bus
and on the way home
in darkness, I told her
how the crowds had been so much larger
so long ago, how you could truly have been lost
for days in the shadow of banners rigged
like sails, how the rulers of my childhood
teetered on the brink and fell.

Indian Summer

I go back to the park
and waste time
with the people who love to.
Our lives spent
for nothing are a bond
and we trust each other.
We sit on a bench and ask
abstract questions:
"why are we still
in infancy." And the acid dealer
pricks up his ears and intervenes:
"Few men know God.
Of a thousand, one seeks.
Of a thousand seekers,
one finds. I myself
fell back into illusion."
And he struts off
making money, while we sit
trusting the little fire in matches
and the hint of autumn red
in the tourists' pastel dresses.

Ten Seconds

At times we woke at an odd hour
and watched the breeze lift the curtains
and because of the silence
this deep in the city
—no church bells, no sirens—
we assumed it was the wind
that precedes the blast
by ten seconds, and we prayed
and waited, then drifted
back to that dream
in which our fathers are not dead.

Isolation in Action

The Old Country

The ice on the river has grown old
and last summer's eddies are fixed
in shallow transparence: a spiral staircase,
the whorl of a thumbprint, a thresher blade,
all existing only in image, as if a cloud's reflection
might conceal a hive of inner corridors, an arch
with a keystone and vanishing threshold: sometimes deep
a fish hangs preserved, sometimes
it's living and flashes and escapes down.
In the farmhouse a woman is sewing,
four children trapped in the corner of her eye.
When they play too close to the banked fire
she whispers No. The eldest has learned
to force her to kiss his hand: he brushes it
on the hot tongs: so when he nears the andirons
No forms on her lips like an ice crystal.
But her hand picks up the stitch obedient
to a perfect will or no will, as if
an apple could fall to earth and glide back
to sky: there is no dust on the dirt floor.
The breaths of the old dog and the baby in the crib
have mixed and condensed and the locks are frozen shut.
The husband has been away at market
eight days, one more than usual,
but the wife knows he will come back
because she has dreamt of nothing
except her sleeping children and a needle
gliding through burlap and an axle
shucking over ruts:

    and the husband does come back
but his face in the doorway is late,
so are his sour kiss and sandpaper beard.
The children shy away, having been intimate
with his silence, having drawn with colored chalk

———————

in hidden corners where his shadow was missing:
he is too like the man they remember
to be the ghostly father they whisper to
at night huddled under a rough blanket:
and the man cannot remember the city
because the words for it are loud and empty.
Asked to describe the city children, he answers
—they're big. The woman stubbornly asks nothing
and hints that a jar of flour has mildewed.
So he patrols his house, opening and shutting windows,
holding a lit lantern to the system of bolts,
poking in cupboards for fresh rat holes.
Before dusk he walks his fields.
When he finds the elders sowing their spring crop
snow is tumbling in arcs of black seed,
the furrow to walk is a lilt in blankness:
questioned as to prices he answers: as always.
                    By nightfall
the pear orchard scarecrow is a gray clump
no different from the fertile starts: he hammers
at the sheath of ice over the ragged hat
and the rhythm of his gestures leads him back
to the meeting in the city, where an organizer
spoke for the abolition of debt and the denial
of adultery, praising civil war and common ownership
of land, even of orchards and pond carp:
but he can find no way to tell it
at supper, facing the elders and the candle
and the children who sit on their hands
and shiver in awe of their own hunger
and their goodness and silence,
so he breaks the bread and says Grace.

Tartu 1939

I danced in a cold hall.
The potted palm clattered.
The bass player craned forward
to blow on his gliding fingers.
The cornet strutted his solo
bundled in a scarf
that lolled in rubato.
The women were round, ageless
in layers of mittens and leg warmers,
and each that I asked
rose almost angrily and performed
with an exhausted grace
but if I tried to talk
the answer was:
                    my husband is on his way.
All night behind the bolted door
we could hear the rumble of convoys,
sometimes an order in an unknown language,
but no one moved toward the window
until dawn when the conductor
stood on tiptoe to peek
through a chink in the shutters:
then he dropped his baton
in a paper bag, waved goodbye, and left
by the servants' exit, and as the band
began packing, the room seemed to fill
with cases and trunks covered with labels
of cities by now imaginary:
only a few remaining couples took advantage
of the silence to practice
the slowest possible pirouettes.

Privates

Against the revolutionaries
our generals kept a stable of spies,
contaminated lovers, helpful theorists,
and even more ardent revolutionaries:
against the poor they had cannon:
against the enemy they had documents
missing key phrases, or hinting
at sudden declarations of peace:
against themselves they had
winter and the admirals and our hate:
against us they reserved a stream of dress rehearsals
for paper massacres, each meaningless without the next:
they fed us lard and piss,
housed us in tents in the snow,
and when we were paraded through town
the population spat on us
and we shook our sleeves and asked them
humbly, *had they heard fresh news from the front?*

The Demotion

The first death I saw in combat
was a body hanging from a tree
with a blue grin and an erection
and as we passed I drew my knife
and cut it down and it fell
behind us. Then I felt the other riders
watching me in silence, a long
cantering stare, until finally
one cleared his throat and spoke,
how the early thaw had ruined the peas
and they were tiny in huge pods,
and after a tremendous pause another
mentioned that the apples
had been dwarfed and sour as gooseberries.
That night in camp I carried out my duties
with the mallet and pegs,
I curried frothy yearlings
and folded tunics along the crease
and no one frowned, but next dawn
I found myself back among the foot soldiers,
the men numberless as waves,
facing superior fire.

The Siege in the Forest

We were camped in the oaks
with dead leaves in our hair
and one of our passwords
was the hoot of an owl
and the other was the syllable: death:
because the enemy outside controlled the paths,
the cooking pots, the supply of flint,
oilstone, salt, paper and thread,
and he had God on his side and was waiting,
distracting himself because only his own
expectation could threaten him now,
but we were mourning our friends
and blaming ourselves for poor timing
and already the internal enemy
was appearing among us,
the one who'd always been there
standing in the door to sleep,
speaking to us in the rapt whisper
of bone chill, consoling us
for having survived.

In the Winter Capital

A vigil flowed from the mountains
and the cities upstream,
merged, convened, and held silence.
We mourners bowed our heads as if
ashamed of our wisps of private breath
and the stutter of our million footsteps.
We cradled blown-out candles, or picked
nubby wax from sleeves. At sundown
I was separated. Instead of the huge banner
slit for wind at the head of the street
laundry arched between lampposts.
A few of the strangers seemed to be marching
with a familiar purpose and despair,
but mostly I met workers home from the mines,
bowlegged, dazzled, laughing, dwarfed
by their own fatigue. I was scared
of asking directions, not knowing
the local dialect, not knowing
the ordinary names of my destination:
only Grave, Monument, Reflecting Pool.
So I slowed my pace, kept the candle
in my pocket like a bottle.
Once a girl skipped up to me
and asked, who are you crying for?
I pointed to the bulge on my coat
where a button was missing; she nodded
darting off, and I trudged on
into the hive of lit windows.

Voices over Water

Voices over Water is the account, in their own fictionalized words, of a couple who emigrate from Estonia to Western Canada in the early twentieth century.

Saaremaa

When I skipped rope before memory
the song was already in my mouth
as the bread was hot on the table
and the sea cold behind the shutter.
I thought I was listening to the whistling rope
and to laughter and my breath, but I was hearing
a force unknowable as my body,
familiar as my father reading by his candle,
and the prayer that summoned this god was:
One And Two And Three And Four And.

*

One summer, the village elder pointed, saying
"don't waste money on a boy, whose voice will break.
Teach this one." So they shipped me to land
and when I came back my girlfriends
were plump and angry and pledged to elders
and refused to speak to me: when I made my village debut
rain staccatoed on the steeple and the audience
fell asleep as if I were delivering a sermon:
they woke long after I'd exhausted my repertoire,
stretching luxuriously, and only because the trade wind
drummed ostinato at the black stained glass window.

Factions

Horsemen came by my house
at night wanting to know
which side I was on.
At first I said: God:
meaning, nothing: but later
even that was not a safe answer.
I said the side of the poor
but that became very dangerous.
I explained I was on the side
of God's poverty but not my own
and against the divinity of the poor
except in my case: but these were not men
given to subtleties: they had ridden hard
and their horses whinnied outside
lathered in the icy wind.

Slow Summer

The war was delayed, so was the truce
that would have concluded it,
the settling of the refugees
was postponed, and in that August
the frontier tangled like our bodies
in love, sometimes following
the river, sometimes swerving
inland across the vineyards
toward the shadow of the cliff
—then we moaned, not knowing
if we wanted a child
or to be free of each other
forever, and the apples thickened
until the branches bowed.

The Marriage to War

I always expected my husband to leave me
because he was the meekest man conceivable.
He sold his fruit trees for my singing lessons,
the quince for the major scales,
the plum for the minor,
then he had to barter his dusty flax
for my arpeggios, and to make weight
he hosed the consignment down.
They caught him and while he was in prison
I learned my first recitative
and all of an aria except one high note.
God knows what they did to him
but when he came back I sensed he blamed me.
He began signing contracts with vague salesmen
from countries that had already fallen,
shipping his contract timber by rivers
charted only in obsolete law books.
He was ruining himself slyly, as with a whore,
but just when he was free, so deep in debt
he held the whole town in the grip of his weakness,
when his worst enemies prayed he would live forever,
the scouts began drifting in from the East.
They built a fire in our rose garden
and pounded on our door, demanding dry kindling.
They surfaced in the market on Sunday
and insisted on paying for every grain of barley
but the face on their coin was Satan's.
They were only the forerunners of the vanguard,
gorged on the endless dales of Karelia,
and what scared me was the camp followers
still a thousand miles behind: but I changed my mind
when I found a buck private hidden
in the coal bin, listening to my scales.
When I threatened him with the poker, he shook himself
like a dog and whispered: Do Re Mi, Mi Re Do,

---

as if it were a language. Then I knew it was time.
I caught my husband as he was drifting out the door,
flat paper roses in his pocket, claiming
he was on his way to feed the pond carp,
and I forced him to load our wagon
with the chest of old love letters, the washboard,
the metronome and a change of linen.
Looking back an hour later, my husband pointed
to a small white cloud and said: "that's our house,
if it were wet smoke from green forest wood
it would have hung in the wind a few seconds longer."

The Occupation

Once the professionals had killed each other
and the conscripts had deserted
the volunteers began to arrive: men who staggered,
eyes merry with wood alcohol,
and sometimes threw away their rifles
because the straps chafed their shoulders.
We could have killed them, sometimes did,
but there were always more: it was futile
as standing in the rain to sponge the damp
off your old cow's back, or trying to fill out
any of the forms of any of our governments.
These new troops were certain they would die,
giggled over it, cared only about committing
enough crime so that God would not forget them
again in the next world, Flies adored them.
Even the scavengers who crept after them
barked orders at them. One time
they marched into the next village,
lined up all the livestock against a wall,
and executed them for violation
of an unannounced noon curfew, firing away
until even the hungriest of the scavengers
could only sell the scraps
for lead on the black market.
They came back, to our village, to apologize.
But by then we were just eyes in the forest,
whispers in an extinct language: we watched
from high in the trees as they dragged out
our old brocade dresses, and stuffed them with manure,
and bowed to worship them: they broke down
our kitchen chairs for crucifixes:
they knelt in the snow and whipped themselves
with our expensive barbed wire, sobbing
God Have Mercy, and when they were seriously bleeding,
when their nude bodies turned sunset colors,

the sergeant slowly shook himself,
took a swig from a private flask,
hitched up his pants, puffed a cigarette
until he stopped shaking, then barked
"eyes right . . . eyes left . . . fall in . . .
attention . . . forward, march."

The Hidden Fighters

We retraced our steps though the signs were bad.
At twilight a huge man stood in the road with an axe.
When he saw us he whimpered in terror and plunged
    into the undergrowth
though we were just two peasants, a child, and a deaf
                horse.
At night we found our moonlit road
obstructed by wheels: wheels of carts, phaetons,
coaches, surreys, toy horses, all frozen.
So we drifted along by the logging paths
that were sometimes just accident, angles
    of snow and windbreak.
Sunrise was black because we were so deep,
the rustle of the owls stopped,
we came upon a child's swing dangling from a branch
and then another and another, a forest of swings.
We found a glass case covered with branches:
it contained an encyclopedia. Then we looked up
and saw the carcasses of butchered deer
lashed to the treetops and painted chalk white
like enormous clumps of snow and we knew
we were in the camp of the partisans
and the silence around us was not ours,
nor was it the silence of fear.

Expulsion

They asked our names, if we were married,
and who were we? They allowed us
to answer the last question with the first two.
Under our breath we were rehearsing, No,
we do not sympathize with the Revolution,
the counterrevolution, God, Satan
or atheism: but they did not ask,
they spared us.
                                    It was almost cruel.
Then we stood in the stunning cold
to wait for our visas in that crowd
of ministers, peddlers, bankers,
judges, thieves, and nuns,
huddled outside the garrison door.

The New World

The dogs barked, but not just at me:
at all the strangers lined up on the wharf,
some in frock coats and some in denim.
Once the foreman came out and pointed
at one of us who wore a leather apron:
otherwise dusk fell and the baying of the hounds
forgot us and became ecstatic and sorrowful
and the tiny windows of the granaries they were
                                          guarding
held the sun and darkened. The wind rose. At night
the foreman's daughter tiptoed out and asked us
what we wanted and we said politely
in all our languages or in mime
Work: and she answered politely
that she could give us bread and even meat
in charity, or a night's rest, as for work
she was just a child and had hardly enough
to tide herself till daybreak.

Alberta

In this country there's a thousand miles
between one milestone and the next.
The wells are so deep you drop a bucket
and lace your boots before it hits water.
Sometimes you see the smoke and lights
of a huge city on the skyline
and you know it's the herd being ridden south.
Then the ground shakes for days
but you hear nothing except prairie dogs
bickering over stones: and this silence
is a strong arm encircling my wife,
protecting her from those strangers
who once were the world.

No Harvest

Anything my husband owns
becomes his manhood: his wheat,
his dog, the shadow of a cloud
the instant it passes over
his stake, a fly buzzing
at the inner perimeter of his doorway:
his manhood weighs on me:
and the drought in the next province
is so fierce, the sky is black
with smoke from precautionary fires.

A Year of Hunger

When the famine came
we ate our seed, our horsefodder,
our chickenfeed, our broody hens,
our milk cow, and then we ate
dust and slugs and hoarded sugar.
We became weak and dizzy and saw
God too easily, in every shift of wind.
At last a neighbor came riding
with a city paper announcing
in banner type FAMINE ENDS.
We saw it was dated a week prior
and a new prosperity was spreading
north with the ground thaw,
the value of land was shooting up
all around us, and that night
we killed the stud bull,
toasted our luck in his blood,
broke a winestem, made love,
woke at noon and suddenly
began waiting.

The Market Holds

We've hoarded our delights
like pennies in a sock
and they're heavy: our children
cry from dreams not hunger.
We weep for those we left behind
to die in our place, our fathers
and brothers, but we also understand
our horse is paid for, and the front wheels
of the buggy, and seven spokes in the rear:
the pots in the kitchen, though not the lids:
the curtains, though not as yet
the velvet ropes that hold them open
so all who pass may know
we're still in love, we work, we lack nothing.

The Shy One

My wife grows foreign as if
each night we pumped
distance from the well,
while the girl I never married
conquers her fear and raps
on my glass at dawn,
trembling in that village lace
of fifty years ago, in her hair
a drifted leaf and a silver comb.

The Last Preparation

The preacher's daughter came to lay my husband out
and I stood beside her wondering if I dared
pay for her labor, until the silver burnt
with cold in my palm: but she flushed,
then sweated with the effort of coaxing him from his
                    trance,
working the corners of the mouth up and pummeling
the eyelids down over that streaked void, even though
I'd wheeled him into the sun three noons running.
When she was gone, accepting nothing, I saw she'd
                             prodded
his limbs into prayer, but to me it looked
like two wrestlers' hands locked in a game
and I knew the right was stronger
so I leaned a little on the left:
then I washed my body and waited indoors
for the footfall of the comforters' horses
plodding on their glass-smooth road.

Surviving Partner

Satan tempted me
to his paradise of despair,
explaining that no one
would ever fathom my grief.
I refuted him, pointing out
that this world is full of widows,
broken cups and cracked mirrors,
and that the body propped in the barn
had been a cheating husband,
a farmer like the rest, not saved
or damned. I was so stubborn
Lucifer grew afraid and left.
Then my enemy was God's mercy
poured out second after second.

Cold Brahms

I dusted my book of lieder with a feather.
It was gray with fungi, glued shut
by cat vomit, and I prized it open
with tweezers in case my rough hands
might pulverize it. I set it
on a music stand made from a chicken coop
and thought how hard it would be and chose
to think how easy it might be
and made myself silent and went
to empty my bowels and looked out the window
and saw the quarter note crows
perched on the telegraph wire
and one half note snowy falcon
waiting: and beyond them
the same blank shimmer over the Great Slave Lake,
the Great Bear Lake and the summits
of the Chenang mountains, where diamonds
crack with cold, and beyond that
the Arctic where ice shifts an inch a century,
and then Russia and the education colonies.
I cleared my throat and tried to put
all this information into the first note:
it was Mi Bemol and came out
a little clearer than I expected, but I knew
it would take me years to relearn even the first
                                    measure
so I cursed out loud and then appealed to God,
but my daughter consoled me, pointing out
this was Canada, there were no Cossacks,
no Germans, no village drunks with guns
and principles, no elders with prize cattle
to die for, nothing
in fact, except that telegraph line
linking frozen seas: so that I might live
as long as I had to.

Mistakes

The complicated passages I master without effort.
I learned the trills and semiquavers listening
to my son's intricate breathing when he was so cold,
newborn in the withered forest. But at the simple
long held notes my mind falls asleep as I taught it to
when anything is prolonged, as it slips into a trance
when the feed falls toward the chickens or the broom
inches toward the pan or sweat glides after fever,
and I drop right back into the old bitter dream
that began in my mother's womb, as if
now were my chance to master my illusion
of always dying, and when I look up
the pianist is staring at me baffled:
I used to swing my fan and stare back
disdainfully, but I've had to train myself
to blush, because he's the only sober maestro
between these plains and the Bering Strait.

Extinction

That fall the wild pigeons passed over us.
I woke and there was a river in the sky and a black
sunrise that lasted until nightfall.
They settled on the shrub I planted
in memory of my husband's fruit trees
until it broke under them. They nestled on the
                                    scarecrow
and stained it solid as a statue with their droppings.
They gathered on the roof, eaves, ledges
and doorknobs and filled the house with a pulsing
as of a great heart outside the body. I fell on my
                                    knees
and prayed: can there be another war more bitter
than the one that destroyed us long ago?
Next day there was no dawn and I knew
this was more than an omen and asked God:
can there be a world more hidden than this one,
sparser, emptier, that they are escaping to?
That night there was no dusk but next day
they were gone and their droppings
had frozen in little walls, like the foundations
of a city still to be built.

Arrival in the City

It starts to rain at the bridge
and by the nineteenth bridge
the rain has turned to snow.
When the Greyhound stops at the lights
there's an empty moment.
She thinks: in a city this big
how will my own death find me?

And if you find me how will you know me
from the other women with parcels
and visas with faded stamps,
snowbound in buses
while the wind whips on roofs?

Then the lights stop changing
behind a wall of brilliant vagueness
and she's neither traveling nor standing still.
She permits herself a brief dream
in which she allows nothing to happen
and when she wakes
they've passed Naptown, Fishburg, Lamp Hill,
and stopped at the corner of Ninetieth and Tenth
and the tenement is larger than any palace.

She composes herself
in the sour box of the elevator
and starts down the corridor.

Each door has a little number
or a numbershaped absence where the tin was stolen
and she smells kielbasa plátanos marijuana and lye:
then she hears the music: polka merengue breakdown
western swing bluegrass cumbia, a phone ringing
on a radio, a phone in a room where a sleeper
is dreaming, a phone in an empty room, a phone

ringing while whoever might answer is busy
peering out the keyhole, and back to fado
sarabande Charleston plainchant hornpipe:
she opens the one door her key will fit
and enters silence.

Inventing Nations

My grandmother's flesh has grown luminous,
cloudy behind her nylon housecoat.
Since her treatments, she can keep down
only Jell-O, sherry, and whipped cream.
She stays up all night watching old movies:
sometimes she loses her temper, turns off the sound,
and hexes the characters in a language
no one in this city has heard of: by day
she stares at the Hudson framed in her window.
She can no longer identify the flags of freighters
and asks me to, but strain as I may
my vision blurs, and she insists, so I wind up
inventing nations: Liguria, Phoenicia,
Babylonia . . . and she nods. On her wall
Kennedy faces Truman but there's no picture
of the child dead of consumption
or the child dead of hunger
or the child who was my father
who succeeded, whose heart failed.
All there is from that world is a locket
showing the infant Mozart playing silence
on a tiny clavichord, behind cracked glass.

Leaving Xaia

The Car Bomb

There was a murder at the corner
and the police left the body
cordoned off, waiting
for superior experts:
detectives, chemists, those who draw
chalk lines. Through the night,
as the mood took us, we drifted back
taking our place in the crowd of spectators
that changed constantly because of the cold.
And the rumors changed, from drugs
to numbers to race. But each witness
wondered at the precision,
almost dispassionate, of that hate:
the body sitting at attention,
untouched face, chest blown open,
becoming familiar as the hours passed
toward dawn, so that sleepless children
ran up to the window, calling
obscene names, until the police flashlight
wheeled and focused on their eyes,
dazzling them, driving them back
to the narrow houses of our street.

These Are Your Rights

The counterdemonstrators were waiting
at the bottom of the street
and their poverty shocked us.
Bricks in paper bags,
bats, hoarse voices shouting
faggots, these streets are ours.
The space between our ranks
and theirs seemed living,
a strip of noon where dust
and blowing wrappers
were imbued with will.
They stared there too,
not meeting our eyes,
as if reading a signal
in that narrowing gap.
We began to sing,
they found a chant,
we struggled to hear their words
under our harmony,
the distance between us
no bigger than a body.
They spat and some of us
who sang swallowed that spit.
They parted, we kept marching,
they were an audience,
as they faded behind us
we could piece together words:
faggots, these streets are ours.
Then we turned in to the green suburb,
the boulevard of carved maples,
plaster dwarves with chipped lamps
painted white, and there
the line of squad cars
parked slantwise was waiting,

the visor raised a bullhorn
into its shadow and the voice
—pure metal—articulated:
These Are Your Rights.

A Pause at Delta Assembly

When the foreman brought my pay
it was sixty dollars short.
I complained, my voice cracked,
he smiled and said,
you must have been sick.
The shop steward advised me,
file a grievance in ninety days.
I told the man beside me
on the line: he put my check
in his pocket, signaled,
               the line stopped,
the crankcases stopped, suddenly
just things, no longer
hours cased in steel:
there was a deep silence,
a force like loneliness,
you could hear flies, high up,
rubbing against the kleig lights:
then the owner came to me
and opened his wallet, saying
I found your missing days.

A Block North of Mercy

I miss the moans
of the incurable ward,
the clinking bedpans,
the radio's consolation.

A younger patient
needed my narrow bed,
tight plastic bracelet
and glass of cloudy water.

Who am I now
without that chart
that dipped and jumped
at the will of fever?

All praise to the mask
who healed me with a knife.
Now I pray for patience
until the light changes.

The Last Husband

I met him at one of those receptions
I haunted after my divorce,
in a district of ballbearing factories,
stockyards, binderies and distilleries:

a man remarkably like me,
perhaps even more exhausted,
nibbling intently on a jumbo shrimp
as if watching a great secret
disappear before his eyes.

Was I eager to be exposed?
My tie was creased and threadbare.
I knew nothing of semi-pro hockey
or put-shares in the bauxite industry.

I had to drink almost as much
to talk to him as once to you,
but the chilled wine was astonishing

and I found myself dreaming of home,
of the white bed and shivering curtain,
the breeze and the mysteries of sacred love:

as I drained my glass
he emptied his, and side by side
we gobbled the calamata olives,
sushi, scones, melon cubes impaled
on toothpicks wrapped in green cellophane,
squid, rhubarb, endives, strawberries:

we spoke softly, like children in a trance,
of the starting lineup of the Harrisburg Huskies,
the vast deserted mines in Zambia
and the movements of money via satellite,

until the bay window darkened
and we saw our ghostly bodies
exchanging statistics, blessing each other,
unwilling to part or pronounce your name.

Final Settlement

My lawyer put his fingers together
and began confiding a strategy
to defend my rights to my child.
As he spoke in a stage whisper,
accenting the names of hostile judges,
my mind went slack and my eyes wandered
to the expensive view:

the park, the wharves,
the cities of Jersey
whose names run together:
Hoboken . . . Secaucus . . . Weehawken . . .

In the afternoon haze, four light planes
were skywriting with exquisite precision
but the wind took their message
and unraveled it like a skein:
a politician angling for votes?
A lover trying to reach a lost one?

Then the attorney coughed
and offered his faintly scented hand.
The documents were drawn and sealed,
that crisp Holland bond
almost tense as living flesh,
a tiny gap marked with a cross
where my name was already written.

The Swiftness with Which Those Cities Fell

1. No Talks

That August, reflections grew very bright
and flickered at the edges
and appeared on land as well as water.

Two faces from the screen
glided through the crowd,
one a father, strict but fair,
the other in shadow.

There were voices offstage
to praise the fire
hidden in reason, the laser,

the wind in the nucleus: other voices,
equally calm, explained the desert,

how waiting here will break a man.

2. A Skirmish at El-Nejd

War to extinction
against a country we've never seen.

The recon flights last forever.
A pilot returns, telling the camera:
"I saw a fire creep up to me.
But I was out of reach."

Reports from hidden witnesses
of polio, cholera,
diseases from other centuries.

The wells changing hands,
then the mirages,
then the smoke.

The line of retreat on fire.

Was it two minds or one
that waited for this
quivering, chose it, conjured it

out of vague documents
and the dazzling heat of El-Nejd?

3. The Air Bridge

We bombed
until the enemy was immortal,
we bombed until he was dust,
we bombed a few more weeks:

our satellites disclosed his trenches
glowing with phosphorus:

was there a mind there
still living, or just a device
trip-wired to return our fire?

4. The Absolute Ruler

If we could rid the world
of that one face

if we could cut it
from the paper
leaving a hole
singed at the edges

if we could block it
from the screen
with a crown of static

if we could turn those eyes
away from us

his secret police could remain in Basra
and his gunships patrol the North.

5. The Human Shield

Why did he put mothers and children
in the air-raid shelter
where we could kill them?

Why did he leave conscript soldiers
to face us, on pain of death,
without armor or water?

Who was he?
A shadow that had crossed a line
between childhood and death?

A voice speaking triumphantly
in an undecipherable code,
promising God's paradise
to those who could hold out against us
until the furnace of summer
and the coming of the great winds.

6. The Will to Resist Must Fade

My great-grandfather combs
in the dim mirror.

The swiftness with which those cities fell
reminds him of something
—he can't remember what it is.
He straightens his cravat.

What he wants we all want.
Unconditional surrender. It is at hand.

7. The Windy Season Offensive

After the parachutists disguised as leaves
and the alleged mugging behind the mirror
and looking down in winter from a glass cliff
and deciding to be happy,
                    everywhere I go
I meet the survivors:
in subways, in museums,
one of them will come at me without swerving
as if to ask for a light, or a cigarette, or news,
and then turn, like a sack of air emptying.

I want to know what you expect from me,
faces that survive me.

8. A Prayer for News

In the middle of a meal
we checked the dial:
without the voice
we had no hunger:

in the act of love
we watched:

sometimes just traffic,
or sports, or weather,

or weather in Baghdad
—sometimes the dreams of experts.

What were we staring at?
Why did we think it was the war?

The Guards

They held my passport
next to the torch
and I felt my features
dissolve in a clear pool
of black ink,
then the background
that had held me stiff
and beaming began to char:
the corporal waved it once
in a rain of sparks
and handed it to me
with a slight bow:
at once I stifled it
against my body,
scorching my last clean shirt.
I was allowed into Xaia.

A Night in Toluna

Always that knocking
at the iron door,
and that voice whispering
what if I open?

Then silence.
A raindrop in the courtyard.
The gurgle of the pump.

A hen rustling
her dusty feathers
in a sleep I can't share.

Again the pounding,
terrified but also
as if there were no one—

just moonlight
and the granite road
climbing to the Cordillera.

Soon I'll hear the heavy bolt
being drawn back,
the moan of the hinge
and the dog barking incredulously.

It will be day, and never again
will I dream I saw your face.

The United States Embassy in Salvador

Under the fifty-foot wall
the machine gunners had us check
our keys, penknives, cameras,
lens cases, metal combs,
then we went through the sensors,
the X-rays, the corridor of pictures
of Jesus and the Beatles, and we sat
in the auditorium while the attaché
explained how the killings
had receded, and unfurled
a graph big as a flag with a black line
plummeting from 10,000 to sixty-two.
He described how the Archbishop died
in infinite detail, then announced
"this world is violent" and the interview
was over, we left relieved
we'd allowed the rage to dance
in the statistics, not quiver
in our voice and deliver
us to him: in the courtyard
the sun sealed our eyes,
the guards counted out
crucifixes, ballpoints,
coins with edges worn sharp,
and we stepped out
into the lines of those who wait
permanently, the widows,
the amputees, the visa sellers,
who parted, as if by instinct,
without looking at us, perhaps
knowing us by scent, or the heaviness
of our footsteps, and let us pass.

The Background Chords Return in Minor

You move through this room
touching one person's sleeve,
another's cheek.
How easily you make us laugh,
coax us to forget the curfew,
make us talk about ourselves
as if we were free.
You know the great exhaustion
that comes from growing old
in a city of shifting alliances.
You understand how sleepless waiting
for something we cannot even name
—a child's voice, a scent on the breeze—
has made us stiff like statues
propped together. For you
there is no more consequence,
whoever has weapons is the government,
and the one you wake with
is the one you love.
Still you forgive our ravenous attack
on the watercress canapés,
our jitters at the faint sirens:
we're condemned to discuss the news
passionately, absentmindedly,
as if the bombings were pure chance:
you know we'll always need the tact
of your supernatural fatigue,
your transparent porcelain,
every modulation of your constant music.

The Checkpoints

At crossroads after crossroads
the military asked you for papers,
sometimes friendly, sometimes begging
for a cigarette, or a coin
in your currency, or baseball news,
sometimes shouting, calling you
whore, faggot, child, old man,
sometimes pointing the gun
straight into your mouth
and waiting, sometimes handing you
pictures of Jesus or revolutionary tracts,
daring you to take them, sometimes
asking you politely to wait
—then the day became a life
already lived, now surplus,
in that elastic time
you felt yourself become a helmet
reflected in a filthy window
while they called into radios
and music answered. Once
they took your papers
and you felt your soul dying
but they brought them back
with a neat stamp: war zone.
Behind their dusty epaulettes
you glimpsed a city
that never quite ended:
shacks full of rusty turbines,
boilers, bits of conveyor belts,
files of old men waiting to vote
or children waiting for milk.
Then open country.
Dusty plains, empty
except for water buffalo
and cinders drifting.

Sun heavy as a tombstone.
You squinted at the ribbon
of red dust and learned
to slow for culverts, thorn hedges,
blind curves, and not to answer
if a peasant waved from the fields.
Suddenly you were in the mountains.
Range after range, burning
as if serenely, in the sky
ranges of twisting smoke.
The road ended. So you waited.
At dusk a whistle came.
An hour later, another.
Then a lamp wavered.
You called your name
as if you were already there,
in that dry riverbed
under granite spurs glinting with heat,
and a silence answered, the first
since you came to that country:
only when dark fell could you hear
the faint crackle of distant fires,
a cricket, a guitar in the valley.
A voice said: come to us.
You obeyed and at once
the children had surrounded you:
they pointed scornfully
to their stumps, their bellies
bloated with kwashiorkor, and led you
to the banquet they had laid out:
pancakes in fat, corn
roasted in its husk,
clay pots of rice, and ordered you
in mime or in whispers:
eat.

The Rules of Paradise

Olmos

A man walks a dusty road
dragging a suitcase.
Sometimes he looks back
and sees a shallow rut
wavering beside his footprints.
A dog howls behind a fence.
The man stops and says: shush.
The dog shuts up.
It has never heard such longing.
Olmos: the first border village.
The guards are sitting on barrels,
playing with creased cards.
My father has brought them
grandmother's lace, a pocket watch,
the locket with the child's tresses,
the diary locked with a gold key.
The visors evaluate these souvenirs
with one eye on their cards.
Olmos: a cider mill,
a tavern, a few porches.
A girl on a swing
watches my father
severely from several heights.
Suddenly she scuffs her heels
and runs in a red gate.
A man comes out—a real father—
and stares at the stranger
and spits: Nothing,
and shouts back at the cinched curtain:
Nothing to be afraid of.
Through the half-shut kitchen door
the smell of bread
reaches like a hand
that will mold me out of ashes.

Childhood and the Great Cities

In the dim room, my father
unpacks his books
and sets them on the dusty shelf
in order of weight.
Marx. The Bible. The Atlas.

He runs a finger
along his knife-edge crease
and coaxes his trousers
onto the clasp hanger.
He will not wake me.

These sheets are stiff
from honeymoon come.
I turn to face the wall.
Lovers moan inside the plaster.

Now my father lies beside me
and clasps his hands
over his pale belly.
In case I can read his mind,
he dreams in his own language.

                                         *

We are still in the middle of the journey
from Alpha to Omega,
Petersburg to Los Angeles,
workers' state to Kingdom of God.

Each city is larger than the last,
each room smaller,
each keyhole more dazzling.

I tiptoe to the curtain
and see a general on a stone horse

and moonlit slums—roofs crisscrossed
by immense names, massed laundry,
towers where every window is lit.

After midnight my father grunts
softly, not to wake me.
Soon he begins talking
in the old language,
haltingly at first,
then in a flood
as tears come back to him.

And I'll sit cross-legged until dawn
to guard him from that stranger
with whom he bargains
in a terrified voice.

Childhood and the Last War

It was being fought in another country,
perhaps another continent.
My father said it could not reach us
except as news—the days were headlines,
letters, telegrams, once a voice
crying in the stillness of the hall.

At twilight my father
ran his fingers through my hair
and told me the count of the dead
as if it were my right to know,
as if that knowledge conferred a power
he could not deny me.

How could I sleep?
The room seemed to swell with light
until I lay in a bed
tucked inside the eye.

My father sighed
and fetched me colder water
without being asked.

He shifted from foot to foot,
not daring to leave
while I faked sleep so coyly.

He whispered the great battles:
Verdun, Thermopylae, Cannae.
And the names of the heroes:
Patton, Achilles.

It would be forever until dark.
In the street, older children
were just beginning to play,
their voices raised in jubilant whoops.
A carousel was grinding out a melody
too slow even to be sad.

I peeked through my eyelashes:
the scallops in the wallpaper,
not just watched but watching back
with a harrowing attention.

My bear with four holes
in its button eyes.

The motes of dust orbiting
in the shaft between the curtains,
each more precious than a world.

The Book of Loneliness

Each night in the leather-backed chair
my father thumbs the gold-flecked pages.
I peek over his shoulder:
the letters are blurred
with spiky curlicues
—Hebrew or Greek?,
the words seem to quiver
of their own accord.

Put it down, put it down!
Come play with me
in the new-fallen snow.
Your huge boot
will cave in my footprints
until no one can find me.

Or let me sit on your knee
while you tell me stories
of the war long ago—
among the million enemies
wasn't there one you killed?

But my father's eyes
never stray from the page.
At bedtime he just points
to the tall black clock.

And when I lie alone
in that dark room
he will come kiss me
and sing me the lullaby
in a small scared voice,
as if it were his secret
that I'll never see him again.

The Next World

I dreamt my father was dead.
I woke and he sat beside me,
reading a book. I watched
through half-closed eyes
while he frowned at one page,
yawned at the next, rubbed his nose,
shuffled out. I heard the fierce stream
of his piss and he tiptoed back
and brushed away a fly settled
in an incised gold letter:

I dreamt my father was hugging me,
when I woke he was dead,
the coffin had already been sealed,
the carpenters were spitting on their hands,
passing around a jar of black wine.
I begged to see his face
but the foreman said: "It's late.
Rub your hands along the grain
and see how it's sanded
glass-smooth: touch the joints
and you won't be able to feel
the seam where the choice mahogany
is spliced to leftover pine."

My Father at Prades

He has left his life
with his baggage in the village.

Now he walks by himself
in the forest at Prades.

A tiny sparrow with a fat chest
hops up and considers him
gravely: he's no longer the enemy.

Under a clump of white mushrooms
no one will harvest
he finds flowers with no names:
a teardrop, a bead of blood.

He stumbles on a hidden spring
and sips a loud rushing voice
and the cold of another planet.

Now he can enter the wild hives
and scoop that cloudy honey
in both hands

and the one who was stung
was a stranger, an exile.

No war, no child, no suffering.

Only the waterfall in the fog.

We Believed in the End of the World

We scrunched under the desk
where we once memorized
the lives of saints and heroes

while the teacher droned on
trying to stay calm
in the face of a bomb
that might never fall.

In that rich dark
we learned how we fitted
boy and girl,
how we were our opposites
and each our own opposite.

Above us the stashed gum
of a generation of older brothers
glinted, amazingly hard:
if we tried to carve a heart
that dark sheen cracked.

We believed this world would end:

like water from the fountain
held in cupped hands,
like chalk dust or the powder
from a jelly donut.

Far away the principal rumbled
on his scratchy intercom,

then nothing, the powerful swish
of traffic, silence, time passing,

the pulse quickening
as if to find a way out

and no world except us.

Scattering the March

I was not beaten
but the boy beside me was.
He broke stride, stumbled,
the sticks circled over him,
corralling him into their world.
I met his eyes and lip-read
"save yourself," a whisper
engulfed in sirens.
                    I slowed down
in an unknown neighborhood,
a street of watch repairers,
tinsmiths, tailors sitting
cross-legged in dim windows
staring at lacquered Singers
like men whose eyes
are lost in a fire,
and I ducked past them
glancing sideways
in deep pity because I'd been
a step away from freedom.

The Portrait

My pregnant wife
is drawing in the front room.
Her soft lead
scritches faintly.
I'm in the workroom
watching snow fall:
magnolia holds emptiness.
She tiptoes in and selects
dressed pine for her frame.
Alternate with the hammer
a small exact silence
falls and rises.
Then the scrape
of Holland paper, and she
will come kiss me,
the wood dust
fine on her hand
where the ring is
already too tight.

The Birth Room

We stare together
at the same fixed point
where there would be a curtain
if there were a window.
We try to breathe in time.

There is a method
to standing pain.
It's breaking down.

I do not suffer.
Still I'm amazed
how soon I'm overwhelmed.

In five minutes
we can call the doctor.

The lamp is dazzling
but there's no clock,
no lock, no mirror.

I keep winding a watch.
The second hand won't move.

A glass of water clouds
where you sipped it
a second, an hour ago.

When the nurse enters
with the stethoscope
it's as if we never doubted
and we hear the heartbeat—

command after command
in an unknown language,
directing us to be happy,
to be mother and father,
to grow old, to be loved,

to wait all our lives
for a single moment.

Only Child

1

I cradled my newborn daughter
and felt the heartbeat
pull me out of shock.
She didn't know
what her hands were:
she folded them. I asked her
was there a place
where there was no world.
She didn't know
what a voice was: her lips
were the shape of a nipple.

2

In the park the child says:
watch me. It will not count
unless you see. And she shows me
the cartwheel, the skip, the tumble,
the tricks performed at leisure in midair,
each unknown until it is finished.
At home she orders:
see me eat. I watch her
curl on herself, sleep;
as I try to leave the dark room
her dreaming voice commands me: watch.

3

Always we passed the seesaw
on the way to the swings
but tonight I remember
the principle of the lever,
I sit the child at one end,
I sit near the center,

the fulcrum, at once she has power
to lift me off the earth
and keep me suspended
by her tiny weight, she laughing,
I stunned at the power of the formula.

Rendezvous in Providence

Perhaps the gods are like us:
a couple breathless on a narrow bed.

They speak in low voices,
watching a fly cross the ceiling.

The self they lost comes back
on the breeze from a rickety fan.

A clock strikes. One touches
the other gently on the wrist.

As they undressed each other
now they dress themselves

in deep silence, and leave us
alone with this clock and mirror,

this love, this fear, these white hairs
tangled in a single comb.

First Grade Homework

The child's assignment:
"What is a city?"
All dusk she sucks her pencil
while cars swish by
like ghosts, neighbors' radios
forecast rain, high clouds,
diminishing winds: at last
she writes: "The city is everyone."
                    Now it's time
for math, borrowing and exchanging,
the long discipleship
to zero, the stranger,
the force that makes us
what we study: father and child,
writing in separate books,
infinite and alone.

The Last Border

The child opens a brass-bound album and asks:
"Are your parents or the pictures dead?
If they're not alive why do they have faces?"
To distract her, I point out the background:
oaks glinting in the twilight
and a road leading there. I tell her:
"That's a grove, perhaps they were resting
in the shade at the center
and that's why their faces
look so blurred; there's a donkey
grazing on grass from before the war,
a crow on a fence, if you look closely
you can see the sentry box they'll pass
to cross the bridge, and if you could read
the labels on their bag would tell you
they've finally arrived at Olmos,
it's 1939, they may escape . . ."

The Bond

You were the only one in that room
who was dead, the only one
with no hope of return,
and I gravitated to you
steadily, negotiating brief conversations
with the drunk sculptor
and the exhausted dancer:
but when I came into your presence
I was shy and chattered
about my career and prospects—
the vanities I'd hated in others.
You were calm and thoughtful,
peeling an orange as you listened,
wincing as the acid bit under your nails,
nodding eagerly when I paused.
You deplored the great rains
that had drowned the winter wheat.
I countered with my list of sacrifices
as if I could bind you to life
by suffering, and you frowned,
you put your hand on mine.
I could barely hear your answer—
I had to read your lips
with that music pounding
in your ears and mine—
but you comforted me, explaining
the power of detachment.
Lowering your eyes, you urged me
to teach myself patience,
to sleep more, to trade wine for milk,
to take care when I left,
given the lateness
and the difficulty of knowing
who rules these half-lit streets.

The Fall

Initials

We'd been drawing in chalk,
amazed they would allow us
to sign the world.

We made the grid for a game,
a ladder to paradise.

I wrote her name.
She entered mine.
I inscribed a heart, she the date.

We'd been given everything:

the little dusty box,
the road stretching
all the way to the neighbor's house,

the threshold, the invisible watcher,
the huge hour until twilight.

Left Field

Told I threw *like a girl*
I waited out in the shadows

while the infielders made spectacular leaps
—by luck or memory of the future?

Some threw like older girls,
some hurled streaks of evening,

all grew equally remote
as night fell and the voices
singing *no batter, no pitcher*
faded under crickets.

I pounded my glove,
spat, dug my cleats
savagely in the sod
and growled *swing.*

Secretly, I was proudest of my skill
at standing alone in darkness.

The Hellmann's Jar

Lucky sealed in a tarantula and a praying mantis.
He had reamed air-holes in the lid.

He invited me.
These are the Gods of War.

The bug eyes ignored each other.
That too, Lucky explained, was deep combat.

We stared and waited.
Sometimes we glanced furtively
at the kitchen clock.

The fighters stood enchanted,
camped in bodies that seemed immense,
gossamer legs arcing
with the contour of the glass.

Later, the question:
how to give them food and drink
without disturbing the trance of strategy?

Lucky blew in atomizer mist.
They would eat each other.

On the third day we woke.
The spider was still alive
immobile in its corner.

The praying mantis had vanished.

A good soldier, Lucky said.
He gave his life.

Paradise

Lucky prized open the capsules.

Feverfew, phenobarb,
rosehip, shark skin,
methamphetamine.

He sifted the powder
on a Polaroid negative.

He weighed the dose
on his mom's scale.

It didn't register,
though that needle trembled
at breath itself.

He gulped.

He looked at me
with bright eyes.

This world was silent
like a clock between ticks.

I was so happy
he hadn't offered.

But did he know
how far I'd traveled
from the immaculate family room—
catalogs on low tables,
white shag carpet—

how old I'd grown
just by watching?

Under the Porch

Lucky peeled the wings
off a fly
and gave them to me,
as Father once trusted me
with the tiny screws
when he fixed his glasses.
But in my cupped hands
they disappeared.
It was a miracle.
We looked everywhere.
The fly buzzed—
how could it still buzz?—
much louder than before.
At last we reconciled ourselves
and knelt with great compassion
and watched as it moved
in an almost line,
then an almost circle,
there in the crawl space
under the huge brushes
rigid with shellac:
and we were rapt
as if we'd found
the way out of loneliness.

At the Stage of Riddles

I tiptoed behind my father
and cupped my hands
over his eyes and whispered:
                Guess Who?

Always he thought hard
and answered gravely:
Eisenhower. Or *DiMaggio*.

And I was happy, knowing
he was safe from my love.

Almost I envied him
the brevity of his confinement
in the unknowable darkness.

An Opening in the Largest City

The lovers look perfectly natural
next to these atrocious paintings
of the Sea of Okhotsk and the Sea of Marmara.
I'm the one who needs a prop,
an invitation or just a wineglass.
I've worked all my life on this mask
of fascinated suffering, still a guard
might arrive at any minute and whisper
and I'd have to nod, summoned.

Occasionally a distinguished guest
pauses to peer at a gilt frame
and murmur: *extraordinary*.

All these seas are dead.
I can see my face reflected
in the terribly thick patina,
and the arc of her cigarette:
the trick is not to focus
on the foreground, the linseed scumble,
the knowing brushstrokes that convey
order, chaos, a misty shore
and the attraction of irresistible winds.

The Stone House at Black River

1
We didn't use the fly
or the little brown circle
under the wine bottle
(though it was half-erased),
we used the Mind—

as if there were no gap
between death and the word *death*.

2
Always soon and mostly never
the cat tipped over the waffle mix.

3
Because we were alike
as two buttons
we invented this great war
between God and Satan.

4
The last sip of wine,
last blowing curtain,
a strand of copper hair drifting
in the breeze from Cape Rosier—
so much love seemed a bad omen
but the last days grew more beautiful
night by night.

5
If marriage solves sex,
what cures marriage?

6
Little door we may open
but only as the breeze.

A Couple in Garden City

I

Great Love, like a hostile parent,
always watched us
to see if our nails were clean,
if there were crumbs
at the corners of our mouths—

imperious Love, irascible,
muttered about a catastrophe
we would never know, close
and remote as a lit window—

you will never know how I suffered
in Logos, because of your ignorance

and we lovers unbuttoned shyly
in the night of war and amazing wealth,
sad for each other, telling each other
little jokes to make it easier,
wanting nothing except twilight:

but that Love always with a project:
the darkest night; sharpest pencil;
softest pillow; cruelest betrayal;

so we blessed each other
in a language we invented,
more silent than thought,
each word backlit as in a dream
where there is no choice but kindness,

and that Love, furious, searched
among the laws for a single name,
erased on the day we met.

2

The rake splayed on the lawn,
a hose glittered over daffodils,
the Brillo pad circled the dish,
smoke hovered above the chimney,
the comb journeyed with many setbacks
through a forest of scented hair
and the voice cried in a dark room.
If we were lost in a second of happiness,
how bright will we burn in paradise?

Not even God may enter the past
yet we sneaked there
hand in hand and carved our names
in the pith of the apple tree.

If loneliness were a taxi,
I'd give it our old address:
1 Pison Drive, a block from Euphrates:

picket fence, gambrel roof,
bent hoop, bug light, dangling tire,
in the garage a bike with trainer wheels,
waiting to take us to our father's mansion.

Custody Wars

One seed of chaos had been lost
in the Motar Galaxy.
If it were not found
the infinite stars
would all implode.

The children sat rigid
in pajamas, transfixed
in that constant shifting gleam:
at their feet a heap of dolls,
dinosaurs, skeletons, small gods,
a king with a key in his spine,
a mound of unopened bills,
roach motels, a little wedge
of mouse poison, gnawed at the lid,

and I stood behind them
becoming used to darkness.
The known stars drew back
like a curtain opening
and swiftly we entered
deep space, pure waiting,
each bound by a cold ray,
each with a finger to his lips,

while in another room a phone
pealed—perhaps the final offer—
faint as all the charms of earth.

The Tower Overlooking the City

I asked: could I become like you
through suffering?
You shook your head.
No.
You looked at your watch.
I wanted to know:
was there a way?
You had no idea.
You leaned forward
and touched my sleeve
with two fingers.
Was this what you had come for,
across that distance
so great nothing could measure it,
not even zero?
I offered you water.
I looked in the freezer
for an ice cube.
I hadn't mentioned food.
Perhaps you were starving?
I heated some broth.
Serenity, I said, serenity—
the chance to think clearly—
the tower that overlooks the city—
you frowned as if my words
contained a threat,
a contradiction to some truth
you had that I did not.

You began your preparations for leaving.
You sprinkled ash on the floor
and wrote your name
and wiped it out.
I reminded you how I'd visited you
in Saint Rose's, bringing flowers,

vitamins, cards, news,
how terrified I'd been
that I might never have the chance
to thank you for the last time—
you smiled wanly.
Your presence here was not permitted.

You apologized and I heard
your quick step in the hall
and the old bitter cough
and I knew you were gone.
The neighbors' argument resumed
behind the paper-thin wall
and the sirens again converged
on an imaginary fixed point
in Flatbush or Central Brooklyn.
I rinsed your cup,
then wished I'd preserved
the pattern of the tea leaves.
Moonlight touched your chair.
For a long time I sat in darkness
remembering the consolation
you had brought to my life.
My clock dial was growing dim—
soon it would be dawn
and the immense searchlights
would slowly become invisible.

The Book of Splendor

1 The Body

I found a dead fly
curled in the tiny print.
I breathed on it gently
so it would not cover
the word *Unknowing*.
I didn't want it lost
outside that text
that spoke so lovingly
of two gates—first Mercy,
then Fear—
that lead to the inner world.

2 The Mind

Detachment, the book says.

If you had detachment
the shock of the fall
would be like words on a page.

Even when you were whole
all you wanted was to heal.
Now study calm.

And I've memorized each page,
the margin stains, the errata,
the foxing, the cunning wormholes,
the colorless thread that holds my place
each night until the last.

At Mary Magdalene

If I make myself still
the voices will pass through me
baffled and feast
on the things of this room
calling the night glass
fool and the light switch
faggot.

Little dusty knickknacks
that I failed to care for
on my journey from home:
postcard from Castine
foxed at one corner,
frayed silk rose
with a rigid serrated leaf,
key, tiny mirror . . .

Tarnished now, eddying
in the whirlpool of judgment:
bad mirror . . . stupid rose . . .

All night I hide
at the confines of my body,
no defense, no resistance,
one finger to my lips
to keep me from answering.

Back Wards

A fly might influence us,
so we would crawl on our beds,
rub our legs together,
hop backward, twitch,
touch our bread all over
without eating it.

If a voice in the corridor
said Good Morning
we suffered ecstasy
but if it forecast rain
we panicked: fatal mistake
a moment before healing.

How we feared the visitors!
—huge clammy hands
sometimes not even clean,
palpating as if suffering
had ripened us like fruit.

Did we suffer or they?
When they were gone
we bragged of them:
their size, heft, hue,
the insoluble love
that drove them to Mercy
instead of bridge or tennis:
how they came to look like us—
a crease between the eyes
that was either sorrow
or a hard presentiment:
the gifts they brought us:
grapes, magazines, many Bibles
differing in key passages,
little empty boxes,

wiltless flowers, ribbons,
trophies for enduring,
for never sleeping,
for constant waiting—

while further in the ward
the real patients lie
who have no names,
whom no one visits,
whose cries you might hear
if the gunplay faltered
on the high screens:

they cry without will,
helpless as passing clouds,
just voices, and we,

we would know them
and cry for ourselves.

At Holy Name

The fatigue of the nurse
waiting with the bedpan,
her mind drifting
to a lover's sarcasm;

the unseen child crying;
the panic of the fly
caught in the embrasure
of the window that does not open;

only these are real:
yet I still feel
my mother's hand
cool on my forehead

and her comb untangling
the snarls of a long dream.

How We Are Made Light

Pity the visitors
bent under shopping bags,
who have kept their huge hats
here where there are no seasons,
who run from station to station
with a question so inconsequential
even we patients smile.

Admire the nurse and the aide
who fill out a form,
one beginning at the front,
the other at the end,
speaking of Bon Jovi;
the doctors, washing side by side,
discussing an even greater doctor;

most of all, revere the orderlies
who have come from across the sea
to wheel us through the corridors
to a place where we will be tested,
where we will finally belong
even more inherently than here,
where we will no longer be watchers
but the matter itself,
flesh and soul transposed
to degrees on a scale of radiance.

Side Effects of Colirium

1
Stifling laughter, but no one to feel it.
We all roll around helpless, doctor, nurse, patient,
like marbles in a bowl—whose joke is this?
The little slice of green grape
suspended in the lime-cherry Jell-O
is killingly funny, and here we are
with our feet in the air
admiring the little pockmarks
in the acoustic tile ceiling—
but they're a riot too!
Pores in Father's nose!
And even the guards
subduing us are giggling,
wrestling us and yet
waiting, deep within themselves,
for a punch line, any punch line . . .

2
And I in your arms again.

A Night at Mount Sinai

1

The voices return
saying "coleslaw" while I'm eating coleslaw:
what's terrifying about that? Isn't coleslaw
shredded cabbage, or did the voices
just explain that? With a little "mayo"?
Or was it plain mayo?
Surely they are gods without souls.
Did they order: Napkin?
Fork? Knife? Why with a knife
when this substance is nameless
and passes through me
as if I were the Kingdom—
and if I resist
there is no I.

2

I invented this spoon.
And this saltcellar—
someone else made it
and punched the tiny holes,
but I conceived it:
I saw it in a dream
and heard the word: saltcellar:
and no one woke me.

The Parasite

The doctor looked angry
and I too began to choke
with rage at those shadows
who take up all our time
with their uncontrollable desire.

The doctor removed his glasses
and began to clean them
pensively with the hem of his gown.
The room became hazy, intimate.
A file cabinet hovered beside me.
The doctor was a small white cloud.

At once I saw clearly:
it was all my fault.
The bitterness, dizziness
in middle age, a fall,
the beautiful work
suddenly turned incoherent.

The doctor put his fingers together
as if they fitted a special way—
a gesture that would take years to master
and there was so little time,
every second was measured—

and he spoke very softly.
I sensed his great weariness.
I wanted to rock him in my arms.

Rest, he said, night after night
of sleep without terrible dreams.
And work. And loved ones.
Patience, said the doctor, barely audible
above the sweet constant music.

Leaving Mary Magdalene

As I was signing out
a guard shuffled up to me
and put his frail hand on my sleeve
asking for discharge papers.
I emptied my pockets.
A snapshot of my child,
sweat-stained, curling inward.
A Victory dime, a Wheat Sheaf penny.
A wisp of thread, a die, a comb.
I looked at him in terror.
He stared back baffled,
angry I had no defense.
A radio was piping in Vivaldi.
I wanted to ask, was it arthritis
that gave him that constant mild tremor
and kept the buttons of his tunic open.
Finally he closed his eyes
and breathed: go,
as if my need were a force like time
and had exhausted him.
I swept up the pennies
and lint from the gleaming counter
afraid to say Thank You
and walked through the winking lights,
the heat shield, the self-opening gates,
into those ice-encrusted streets
where I first learned to be no one.

Burnt Island

Ruth

The face on the flyer
was serene as a god's—
below, a phone number
and scratched note:

even if you just glimpsed her,
even if you're not certain.

I bowed to that stare
and flinched at a smudge
where the invisible hand
pressed too hard.

At the curb a rhinestone purse
still held a thimble and a token.

I tripped over two votive candles.
One flame guttered. I knelt
but the wick curled into itself.

That night it rained, you could no longer
smell the steel burning.

When I came back to Union Square
the face was everywhere,
on a red construction cone,
a lamppost, a rental van,
safe in a maze of faces

but the woman had faded—
a cloud with a smudge
where I had seen hair,
the pearl necklace
a string of blobs:

you could still discern
the hand's tremor
but the words had fused
to a solid block:

even if you just glimpsed her,
even if you're not certain.

The Reunification Center

We brought pictures of the missing,
held gingerly, by the cropped margins,
as if the eyes were scalding: or food:
steaming casseroles without ladles,
though the night was mild: Evian:
M&M's, which we tried to hand out
in that cordoned-off street
where an ambulance chugged empty:

and each stranger refused, a little pained,
no, no, I'm here to help: we offered aspirin,
stock certificates, a child's rocking horse,
a teddy bear with an empty eye socket,
but no one consented to receive that treasure:

a doctor ashen with fatigue shouted
into a cell phone, shaking it
when it didn't answer, a digger
dozed hugging his shovel,
a survivor, mesmerized by the portraits,
stunned at their beauty, compared them
scar by scar with the faces of the living.

Searchers

We gave our dogs a button to sniff,
or a tissue, and they bounded off
confident in their training,
in the power of their senses
to re-create the body,

but after eighteen hours in rubble
where even steel was pulverized
they curled on themselves
and stared up at us
and in their soft huge eyes
we saw mirrored the longing for death:

then we had to beg a stranger
to be a victim and crouch
behind a girder, and let the dogs
discover him and tug him
proudly, with suppressed yaps,
back to Command and the rows
of empty triage tables.

But who will hide from us?
Who will keep digging for us
here in the cloud of ashes?

A Walk in Giovanna's Park

Under the immense elm
the children are no bigger than children.

How can anything live
with the heart carved in it so deeply?

The old couple eating saltines
look like twins in the half-light.

A firefly sails past,
the first since we met.

I pull a gold thread
unraveling from your sleeve.

We step carefully here.
The glowworms have begun to flash,

beckoning us to a kingdom
our arrival will destroy.

Don't you know that lovers
like to imagine eternity

while a sparrow pecks at candy wrappers,
staring sideways fiercely?

Lovers have to rest from each other
but there's nowhere in the world.

Even the grass is singed.
Even for the fat white ducks

with painfully orange feet
it's so complicated

_____

to be given a crumb.
Under the immense elm

children are playing with darkness
as if it were clay,

and they've made two small gods
who can't leave each other.

Home

1
You winced in the rocking chair,
waiting for your water to break.
I paced the outer edge
of the raffia carpet.

A radio was playing,
as if there were still news,
traffic, war, sports, weather,
in that huge country before dawn.

But we couldn't break our trance.

Saint Luke was nine miles away.
Sirens peaked and diminished.
We couldn't hear them.

Our blood hammered in time
to the pulse in the other heart.

2
We bundled the newborn
over the doorstep
into the white room
we'd dusted so carefully.

We sat on the bed,
snow on our lapels,
while the child slithered between us
with a swimmer's wriggle.

Then one boiled water, one swept,
one wrapped duct tape
around the cord to the lamp,
one counted pins,
one folded diapers,

in absolute silence,
not even terrified,
as if we were in command,

and after a few days
the invisible snow stopped,
music resumed
behind the paper-thin wall,
traffic roared again,

and always, one held the child,
safe on that journey
away from the body.

A Hike to Little Falls

I

The shell had hardened
and the chick could not hatch
though we sensed its heartbeat
in our cupped hands,
imperious, panicked.

Should we shatter
that delicate casing
scored with faint runes?

Already it smelled of us.
The flock would shun it.

The other eggs glinted,
icy in the toppled nest.

We felt our own pulse
advancing with the same wild purpose
as the heron crossing the river.

2

It was a taint in the rain,
a sweetness in the water,
something else we forgot
to discuss as we climbed here

past Chaux Springs and the Fire Pond,
breathless, exultant, watching
worked land reveal itself,
and above, the false summits,

3
though we packed so carefully:
waterproof matches, compass,
flashlight, freeze-dried rice,

the map carefully sealed
and memorized in two minds.

The Marriage in Canaan

How the dog loved to chase his ball
even in the rosebushes
where thorns tore his coat.

How there was another life.

That long summer
a bee circled our house
diligently, like a toy airplane.

It happened that the child
unhooked her swing
and carried it away
in the crook of her arm.

Happiness undid us.
We wanted to live on a road
exactly like this
but seen from a distance—
the Frisbee in midair by day,
by night the books massed
in their fiery window.

Our gravel driveway
seemed to repel us,
pushing us gently up.

Once the dog found a dead bat
and pawed it gently,
puzzled for a second, then certain
when he rolled the torso over
and saw a cloud of tiny wings.

The child spread thimble cups
on a towel under the elm
and filled them from a broken pot.

Perhaps she was inviting the mind
to sip, one finger raised,
and never thirst again.

Soon it was dusk, she slept
guarded by a little white cloud
in a corner of the mirror.

Night fell like a leaf
and we lovers crept
into those huge names
—wife, husband—

drew them up to our chins
and woke in Mother's house
in Father's orchard.

Then the mockingbird called,
sick with loneliness.

Space Marriage

1
Our starship blew up
between Alpha Centauri
and the Second Quadrant
but we could not die
because we had stolen
the god's codes:

so we kept traveling
deeper into the future
just ahead of our bodies
and when we had sex

we felt ourselves scattering:
there in the galactic cold
where the immense numbers
begin to rotate slowly

we put on the robes
of the night sky.

2
An alien had imprisoned me
in that lunar module
that was just the thought
I and he fed me
what *I* would eat
and mated me
with the one *I* loved:

strange ordeal
there in the Second Quadrant
in Spica's radio shadow
where the gravity of time
pulls dreams from a sleeper's mind:

bitter confinement
naked on a falling stone.

3
We built robots who built robots
that had a little of our hesitation,
our fatigue, our jealousy,
our longing for Alpha, peace, nonbeing . . .

They covered our long retreat,
those machines, that looked
like can openers or outboard motors,
but with the guilty air of husbands
and the god's fixed stare.

4
It was a system.
We loved each other,
the war began on Vega,
we watched the hurtling lights,
and the silence drained us.

5
Out of spit and dust
we made two lovers
who set fire to the earth.

Origins of Desire

After Lynn Margulis

1. Anima

This is the groundwork:
autopoiesis, constant creation
of the self from sunlight.

But gender varies like the breeze
and sex like tides.

Thousands of quasi-sexual fathers
might fuse and form our body,
just visible on a net-veined leaf.

We might cannibalize each other
and the indigestible rind
become the partner.

Or we might trade
genes for *male* and *female*
like beads or playing cards.

But we are each built of water
locked in a membrane.

The same comet-tail sperm
in starfish, ginkgo, and human.

2. Red Giants

Hydrogen caught fire
in the forge of the nebulae
and fused to carbon—

our element, pliant,
ready to combine
with any foreign body:

magnesium, calcium, contaminants
released in the great explosion
that lit the sky like a match

before there was a mind to understand
the advantages of annihilation.

3. Archean Microbes

When the dust cloud
rolled back from earth
we died of radiance—
the sun burnt holes
in the inmost braid of DNA.

Light-nourished, light-poisoned,
we migrated into rock
or traded little damaged pieces
of self between each other,

enshrining separation inside us,
creating the blueprint
for an absolute stranger.

4. The Unlit Room

The mind is a story
that found a way
to tell itself—but who
is the confidant, who
the eavesdropper,
who gropes for a switch
along this invisible wall?

In our narrow bed
we hear the catch
of the other's breath,
faint Muzak, an ice machine,

a late goose honking
toward the idea of south.

Between five and six
we whisper our presentiment—
great herds going blind
in Patagonia, a moth species
extinguished at every breath.

We exaggerate a little.
Those extra zeroes
hold our reprieve.

Perhaps it is too late
and we can still make love
and catnap toward dawn.

But even if we close our eyes
we are still married.

Diaspore
Winged Seed

There is a barrier
that locks me in.
I must endure this sleep
until what seals me off

is burnt, frozen, exposed
to axe blow, erosion, rain,
noon, twilight, starlight:
then I will flower,

everything in me—
triple-folded leaf
of the female organ,
leaf-shoot of the male,
whorled together
like petals in bloom—
will be explained
as if by a voice:

now I must pass
unknown to myself
through the belly and gut
of the northbound sparrow.

Hymenoptera: The Ants

for Deborah Gordon

1
They say we are descended from the wasps.
Can't you feel it?
Once we had a house in the sky
and swooped with a terrifying drone.

Now we are sentenced to this silence
in which our acts become our language.

We carry the bodies of the dead
into the underground hives
and keep our paths swept.

We walk the wilderness
in broken circles
searching for the seed
that contains tamarack, Burnt Island,
the high crests flashing with evening.

Since we lost the Kingdom
to time alone, we make ourselves
always purer, more obedient
to the will (we have no tablets),
carving our doors and lintels
deeper underground.

2
There is one who is huge,
and stoops, and counts, as if
those zeroes were the seed.

To baffle him
we make subtle mistakes—
we entomb a fleck of dung
among the fathers, or wrap mica

---

in strange paper shrouds
and tend it like pupae.

3
We build a city, and after five years
and many dynasties, unbuild it,
and erase our complicated scents
so the earth smells just of rain.

We send our Queen
on her wobbly flight
with her entourage of suitors—
tiny jawless males
who will never eat in this world—

we who have wings only in death.

4
Our wars are fought in the desert,
without mercy, but somehow sleepily—
perhaps the sun makes us drowsy?

The plan is, we grip the enemy
with our jaws below the waist
and try to saw him in two.
He reciprocates.

Sometimes he dies
of thirst, loneliness, distance from the colony,
and we must return to our duties
with those mandibles gripping us,
without anger, or with the anger of the wind.

This is the whole problem of victory:
the severed parts go on thinking.

5
The fire ants have built an empire
high above us.

We know their generals—
Arcturus, Aldebaran—
and their pupae, the Pleiades.

For a thousand generations
they have planned to invade us
from that golden hive.

And we have built an absolute weapon—
silence—when it is perfect
it will abolish them
and the earth, and the kneeling watcher
whose lips frame such immense numbers.

We have wings in death.

Six Red Spiders in the Elm at High Falls

How to describe the web?
It is already in our minds,
already our minds—
how we know ourselves
and imagine knowing ourselves.
As you might dream your universe
no bigger than a fist
at the instant of origin
and ask: *what surrounds it?*
—so the web is our choice.
It shines in midair.
We may walk across it,
immune to its suction
and secreted poisons.
It trembles, like us,
its principle is *give,*
the prey is the center
but when he struggles
he winds himself deeper
sending a message
which reaches us
as we are building the next web—

so days, clouds,
the breeze itself,
are just a voice.

Separation at Burnt Island

Brothers and sisters, who live after us,
don't be afraid of our loneliness,
our dented Wiffle ball, the little kerf
the dog chewed in the orange Frisbee.

Don't grieve for our kite; not the frayed string
that clings to your ankle, not the collapsed wing.

We lived on earth, we married, we touched each other
with our hands, with our hair that cannot feel
but that we felt luxuriously, and with promises.

We made these bike tracks in the sand
—don't follow them—and this calcined match head
is the last statue of our King.

We lived between Cygnus and Orion,
resenting the blurriness of the Pleiades,
in a house identical to its neighbors—
stepwise windows, ants never to be repelled,
TV like a window into the mind
that can't stop talking, redwood deck
facing the gulf.

Everything was covered with sand; the seams
of the white lace dress, the child's hinged cup,
the watch (even under the crystal), the legal papers.

We were like you, or tried to be. We divided our
                         treasures
(a marble with no inside, a brooch from Siena),
signed our names with all our strength, and went home
in two directions, while the marriage continued
without us in the whirling voice of gulls.

Brittle Star

1
I feel the soft tug
of the starfish—I know it
by its gentleness—

but it persists
longer than my closing muscle
can keep my clamshell shut.

2
Then that stomach enters
and consumes me: I am the starfish.
Cut off my arm: it grows back.
When my center hardens

3
I am the brittle star
fossilized in basalt
a thousand thousand years ago

before the great nets
began drifting untended

and the nine-mile line of hooks
uncoiled as a sign
that you discovered immortality.

The Granite Coast

We are like you
because we scrape these boulders
with sharp coiled tongues
which we unroll progressively
as our mouths wear out:
when you open us
you find the cliff inside us
though we are tiny as an eyelash;

we are like you
because we are born by the billions
and float into the open ocean—
as if we were entering
our own plenitude
which is the certainty of death
and the slim chance of sunlight—
and the ones who never return
are the faint roar
in a sleeper's ear;

we too make little threads
mysteriously in our genitals
to hold us to the ledge,
and in our nests we weave
mica and our victims' bones;

we are kin to you
because the great tides
advance and retreat inside us—
though you may call it salvation
or adaptation, it is a circle
in which the living and the unliving,
the souls and anti-souls,
grow their intricate spiral shells.

We are I, I, I—
there is only one of us
and with our frail tentacles
we build the dawn sky.

We are helpless on this sea
full of thinking knives
and coral shards nibbled
by ravenous flowers.

We wage war on ourselves
and drift through our armor
like cloud shadow.

We graze on each other
and the limbs grow back
secreting dark sugar.

The gull will destroy us
and the plumed worm Amphitrite
make a home in our eyes.

Yet our bodies are shaped
exactly like the resting place,
we fit in each other
like silence in desire,
we live another second
or much less, less than a blink,

until the code comes to know itself
and the mind dreams another mind
that will survive it
there, in the bright curtain of spray.

The Border Kingdom

Ben Adan

The American commanded me
in gestures, dig a hole.

He tossed me a shovel
but the blade had dulled
and the haft was splaying
so I had to rein in
that strange wild energy
as I opened the earth
to my shins, then my knees.

At thigh depth I found
a layer of black loam
and a tiny blue snail
that seemed to give off light.

The agent called my name.
High above, he mimed
a man kneeling,
hands clasped in prayer.

He must have knelt himself
because I felt the muzzle pressed
against the shallow furrow
behind my left earlobe—
a part of my body
I never knew existed.
He pulled the trigger.

    But I know
it is just a technique
to soften my resistance—

perhaps in a moment
he will lift me up
and hold me trembling,
more scared than I
and more relieved.

In the Hold

After an unmeasured time as a stowaway
in the stifling void, listening to the waves,
the rats, the grains of wheat settling,
my father heard church bells
and knew he'd come to port.
When they rang past twelve
he was sure the war had broken out,
the world war that had been expected
all through childhood, for so long
tailors adjusted their chalk lines for it,
painters shaded it into the middle distance
like an unknown primary, preachers exhausted
the endings for their sermons:
now my father in the dark cubbyhole
that might be endless, or just a hair
larger than his ungrown body,
counts the coins in his sack,
the stitches in the gunny weave—
he takes his pulse, then having
no more real things, he counts
the members of his family, the chimneys
of his village, all the days
of his life in the old country.

Exile's Child

I asked my father
permission to kill a fly.
I came back and asked
—could I kill another?
He thought for a while
and said—No. Evening was taking
the sting off a family outing.
Along the beach, cousins
were charring meat. The waves
were turning an intense No-color.
I asked, was he in combat
in the old country? He said—No.
Then I was enraged at him,
feeling he was asleep, like the sand,
like the striped umbrella whose shadow
fell at right angles to night,
like my serious brother toting sums
in a leatherbound ledger. The flies alone
were awake, and their drone,
fainter than surf, was audible
only when I knelt and held my breath
stock-still by the banked coals.

The Prize

When we came to the summit,
our father had one grape left.

We said, divide it.

But he refused.
He'd give it to the hungriest.

We fought then
on that narrow ledge,

the vineyards tilting
far below us—

who was most bereft,
loneliest, furthest from home.

As we rolled in each other's arms
we glimpsed a vacant sky,

the mountains of the border
that shine with their own light,

and the familiar dust
glittering with sweat.

The Anti-Death

In case we might lose Roger Rabbit
our mother bought three surrogates
and locked them in a drawer
high in the linen cabinet:

so when we left him
as if by accident
on a swing in the snowy park—

when the older children wrestled him
with shouts of joy from our embrace—

when we dropped him in the icy lake
and the rowboat would not turn back—

she produced him: here is your love
who was not vanquished but only sleeping
in paradise, in the white of the eye,
in the loneliness between words.

Sacrifice

How angry we were
at the stuffed bunny
for making us love it
night after night.

We ripped off an ear,
tore out the stuffing,
scattered it in handfuls,
prized out an eye
to roll in our palms.

The back, that we had never seen,
shone just as bright
as the staring pupil.

We licked our fingers
and teased the empty socket.

Night fell.
We listened for footsteps.

When they came
they were the same as ever,
just the blood beating in the mind,
but the silence was utterly new.

We entered it
as you might sneak through a door,
answered it, as if it were a voice—

yet it was just silence
and we could no longer change it
by laughter, tears,
or any silence of our own.

August Snow

Our father wanted to climb Mount Moriah
and we refused to go
unless it was understood
we were going against our will—
unless we could climb by suffering,
dragging ourselves step by step
through the boxwood glade,
withheld birch, glinting ash, oak bent
to the will of the south wind—

that was our secret,
denial, denial, we were children,
above all we wanted to be with him
above the tree line where the lakes
are dark as the pupil of the eye
and hold massive unmoving clouds
and the mouths of silvery wary carp.
We wanted to descend to the valley
at dusk, and shit and wipe ourselves
on the fat rhododendron leaves—

but he would not let us go
unless it was in delight
so we watched him
trudge off in the dawn wind,

all day we stared
at that faint snow-dusted peak
sometimes hidden by clouds,
sometimes a cloud itself,

and when night fell
it was just darkness
and no longer contained him.

Canaan

How the mind wound up the doves
and sent them volleying
over the shepherds' low fences.

When the tap leaked
the mind said *drip,*
if a dog barked
the mind murmured *echo,*
and when the lovers moaned
the mind gasped a name.

Mount Moriah hovered
like a cloud in the north.
The river glinted like a hinge
long before daybreak.

Abraham had lent us that stone house
with warped blue shutters.

In his dusty pear orchard
ladders were nailed to every tree.

We were voices then—now
we're signs on the blank page.

Lament for the Makers of Brooklyn

I

Where is Policastro the locksmith now?
Half-blind, he wore two pairs of glasses
held together with duct tape,
and arranged hasp, tongue, eye screw
on a deal table—everything ordered
by resistance, scrim of rust,
flange, interlocking wheel,
name, distance from the body:
afterward the key turned
for you but not for me.
He charged us $11.39.
We tipped and he smiled bitterly.
Perhaps he would have smiled the same
if we'd paid the flat amount—
perhaps he had a bitter smile—

Simon his cousin fixed the windows,
assembling mossy torpedo-shaped weights
and flat-linked chain spliced to steel cord,
beveled panels of the embrasure
that fitted into themselves
to make a plane, a sheen
over invisible labor—later
the window lodged at a cant
for you, and for me slid open
on a street of moving vans.

Mr. Fuchs with his green wrench
consulted a brass thermometer
and opened the hydrants in the great heat.
He stood behind the plume of spray
as with a young bride in a lace veil—
where are the children who ran after Spaldeens

and found them floating toward Africa in the gutter,
glinting with gasoline rainbows?

Where is Vera B. Wick
who raised Clarence and Latisha
in a room no bigger than a white glove,
and never looked up from Revelation
during the war against fear?

What became of Clarissa Green
who organized Blue Forge,
preaching to Croatians
from a dictionary in her lunch box,
bargaining with Yemenites
via a Berlitz phrase book wrapped in foil:
shouldn't this life be easier?

Diagnosed with M.S., she took on Bridal Shower
where no union had ever been allowed,
where the carders drool from mercury—
she marched straight up to the guardhouse
and announced *I have an appointment.*

What happened to Sister Violet
who drew pyramids on the chalkboard,
her hands shaking with desire
for a lover dead at Khe Sanh?

Who remembers South Wind, the numbers runner
who came to me in the men's room
of the He's Not Here Cafe
and told me, zipping and buttoning,
I'm going to meet the Sweet One?
That winter he was found
in the trunk of a green Impala
on an access road in the marshes.

Where is Thelma, who owned the pigeons
that made enormous whirling obelisks
and spires, only to disappear
with a single will, toward Bayonne?

2
Once I met a crossing guard from the old neighborhood
at a side table in Starbucks.
She blew on her steamed milk
and tapped her fingers to NSYNC.

Once I met a pipe fitter
who had invested in Power Disk
and made a fortune, and lost it:
so deep in debt he still walked
with the wary nonchalance
of a poor man become the center of the world—
he wore a belt with a mother-of-pearl buckle
and his initials wrought as twisting snakes:
he confided to me, perhaps this was the afterlife,
surely he died from a stray bullet
in that year when the children
began crying for bottled French water.

3
Remember how we lay in the great heat
in our walk-up on Seeley Street
between the immense park and the huger cemetery?
The neighbor's radio played *Fearless Heart*
but whenever we tried to listen to our own music
a plane passed, circling La Guardia—

how desperate we were to sense a shift in power
in the mourning dove's quavering voice,
a new age in the humming clock—
Kennedy, Johnson, Ford, Carter,
Reagan, Bush, Clinton, Bush,

constant whoosh of traffic
passing to the Island;

as if even our bodies, naked, linked
by a stray arm, were time,
and the candor of our love
confined us in childhood.

4
Last night I met the knife grinder
whose cart with its infuriating bell
jolted among the elms
riddled with lovers' names
in the dead of summer,
so that wives left their dark houses
and came to him and offered
the carving knives from their trousseaux—

and he described to me, with a flicker
of his tiny nicotine-stained hands,
how he cut the little holes in the straw hat
so his horse's ears would be comfortable,
and how he honed the blade
so keen you could not feel it cut.

Rosal

1 The Visit

Many identical metal detectors
and the guards in strange moods.
One cups a hand for your change,
lets it spill, and fingers his gun
while you bend to scoop up pennies.
Another is reading Revelation
and waves you on without a pass.

Is it your shoe that triggered the beep?
You will pad in socks, a yellow nail
poking from the seam.

You will walk these dim corridors
while a megaphone calls your name
gently, then in anger, then panic.

Still a trustee will usher you
through ribbon wire and sensors.

And there in a floodlit cell
Rosal is drawing keys
on a scrap of paper—

ancient keys, to enormous locks,
though here the doors are opened
only by a beam of light.

2 The Record

We made a chapbook
and called it My Life
(underlined twice)
(nothing happens after prison)
but the staples were confiscated

—weapon, weapon—
and held in a safe at Command:
there the brassbound book
lies open to a marked page.

3 Parole

Three months I practiced
the reunion in Rego Park:
it happened exactly as in dreams:

a kiss, the promise,
the red-check tablecloth,
the cat watching indignantly,
a candle, the deep kiss,

except we had a few sips of Hennessy
and her brother came by
and commented on punks from prison.
The cat slithered under the credenza.

By daybreak I was back at Command
staring at the whitewashed wall,
hearing myself talk
loud, louder, softly,
then never again.

4 Incident at Ira Cross

It hurts to see it
even with the white of the eye—

everything has a beginning and end
except the beating—

but a roll of toilet paper
sails blazing over the grillwork,
splaying in midair:

even in Section Eight, Isolation,
someone unknowable owned a match.

5 Lockdown

A glove searches the anal cavity.
Is there really a drug
this bloody, or a weapon
so infinitesimally small?

6 Male Minor Detainee

Rosal hung himself
on Rikers Island
with a nylon sock—

how could it hold him
so securely in death
when the whole block shook
with the roar of jets
circling La Guardia?—

to be free and walk
without meeting men's eyes
across the bridge to the city.

The Shelter

You breathed in my ear
and we began waiting,
invincible in our armor
of light sweat.

There in the sub-basement
we kept a water bed,
a radio, nineteen dented cans
of Del Monte wax beans,
the coil to a flashlight,
an atlas and a diary.

We missed each other
most when we came—
then we rolled apart
fingertips touching,
and practiced being victims
of a war in the mind.

How we loved that world,
its smell of must,
its darkness, its single light.

Autopoiesis

A little evening crept
into the poet's Bausch & Lombs;
he polished them
with a chamois scrap
until they were invisible.

He took a sip of Perrier,
admiring his breath
in the vinyl cup.

This next fragment, he said,
is longer than life itself,
but it is the shortest lyric
I ever conceived.

So the voice engulfed us,
whirling us to the past;
when silence claimed us

we waited in that endless line
to grace our crisp new books
with the fissure of his name.

As we inched forward
we touched each other
on the thigh, the cheek,
almost by accident,
as if to remind ourselves
how it had been to be alive—
pure fire.

We admired the halo of down
around that august backlit ear,
the fury of the blue-veined hand
scribbling *self self self,*

and we whispered *love your work*
to the rain in the empty street.

Late Summer

When the rain woke me
I no longer knew
and had to remind myself:
this is darkness,
that is the wineglass,
this is the blowing curtain,
that's the immense city,
it's late in my life
but early in August,
this is my wife
naked in my arms.

Picnic by the Inland Sea

We understood we were hurtling into space
at eighteen miles per second, clouds of atoms
charged and polarized, each alone
in the abyss, and you wore your summer dress.
The light under the poplar was mottled
but the shade of the pines was feathered.
We were bundles of self-canceling voices—
flight and response, punishment and reward,
hostile adoration, panic and certainty—
from long before the Bronze Age,
yet we made our own promises
by suppressed coughs or sneezes
and sat a little apart
but sometimes our eyes brushed.
We sipped Montepulciano from a paper cup
until the bottom darkened
but still it was not evening,
still the world was ending,
always we resented the breeze
for choosing and marking us,
still a song too short to sing
moved two famished sparrows
like pawns from branch to branch.

Parousia

When we were in the same room as the gods
there was little to say.
Do you like twilight? Do you need the touch
of the other's body—the absolute other?
Mostly we stared at their wingtips
which were burnished
and stamped with strange almost-holes.
How could they stand the suffering
of the fly trying to walk
across the sheen and camber
of a brimming Campari glass?
It would happen to us,
but it was they who had to watch
and watching is hardest.
Only a breath away,
they showed no desire to vanish
though the silences that opened
were volatile as the shadows
of the last exhausted dancers.
Which do you prefer—time or lightning?
We could hear the clink
of the chandelier trying to work its way
loose from the vaulted ceiling,
a cello tuning sharp in an inner room,
and curried almonds being gobbled—
that was us, our voracity,
but the gods said nothing:
their politeness is like their love:
glass wall between us and midnight.
We pitied them. It is not safe
on that side of eternity.
Worse than watching is waiting
while the waiters sweep up the party hats
and dark lights of snow
tumble in the tall gilt-framed mirror.

After a Bombing

1
Lovers who had separated
asked *are you OK?*
and reconciled.

Fathers who had abandoned
their children whispered
Thank God you were in Queens.

The man who was late
because of a lost key
felt good fortune on his shoulders,
a tower he'd have to carry,

the woman who called in sick
wandered deeper into fever,
looking for suffering,
for a spring to drink from,

2
and the children drew the plane,
sticking out their tongues, pressing
hard with crayons, never looking up,
as if they'd seen it all their lives:

the tower—a huge box:
the fire—an orange flower:
God—a face with round eyes
watching from the margin:
the sun with nine spokes:

the fireman in his smudged hat
running with outstretched arms
up a flight of endless steps
that veered suddenly off the page.

The Missing

We filled the streets,
squinting upward, shading our eyes,
searching for the towers,
or more planes, or rescue choppers,
and a great silence built

until a girl whispered, *blood*.
She asked her lover to stand still,
used his back for a drawing board
and wrote on a paper bag
Give Blood—instantly

a line formed, then many lines,
twelve blocks east to Bellevue,
eighteen north to Saint Vincent.
We chose one and waited,
gossiping with our neighbors.

We had a place, a function,
something invisible inside us
was needed desperately; we watched
with envy and deep longing

as the rare blood types
strode toward the head of the line
calmly, swinging their arms,
commandos to the rescue.
Then the word came back,
     no wounded.

A Child in Brooklyn

She stood on the dictionary
to reach the mirror
and whispered to that white cloud
look: I'm me.

In another room
her father licked his finger
to leaf through a divorce decree
with nineteen codicils:

as you were before:
independent lives:
child remains happy:
time is divided in two
but child stays in one body:

independent lives, happiness:
why didn't we think of that
before it became law?

In another room
her mother in a large white hat
was packing a valise,
thumbing through postcards,
throwing out an ocean liner,
keeping a waterfall
with an arrow and the words
wish you were still here.

The huge books had been sorted.
The ones with sad endings would be kept
because the settings were so beautiful.
Ischia, Bari, the vineyards of Zion.

Never before had the city been so vast
or the war so remote
or the bombing so precise.

It seemed it had already happened
and been encoded into computers
but no, it was just human life,

if you thought *up* you rose
on tiptoe and *down* you huddled
on the buckling lino.

If you thought *sparrow*
a small shadow darted by
self-important behind the frosted glass
but if you thought
here I start it was over.

So the child drew the letter *I*
in the heart of the cloud
and there she saw a fiery counselor

who shines now she and we are gone.

Love in the Last Days

Love in the Last Days reimagines the Tristan and Iseult myth.

The Grail   *Tristan*

We subdued a village at the edge of Morois—
a toothless hag scraping a bloody sheepskin, a cripple planing
a board of knotty pine, a child plucking a crow, a few girls,
dizzy with hunger, stumbling in the fuller's ditch,
sweat sticking burlap dresses to spindleshanks.

How their dogs' eyes widened when we came riding out of the brush,
out of the play of light and shadow, with our crested plumes,
Toledo steel and argent-gules escutcheon.

We lined the men at spearpoint and asked: have you seen the Grail?
And they asked: what Grail? We were at a loss there.
It was Iseult's obsession and our desire to be perfect for her,
to be good on the bloody earth, so that God would love us
and lift that long stalemate: death without end, or grace.

Allegedly it was a jar that held Christ's blood, now empty.
We cupped our hands, describing it, and the manants pointed
                              vaguely.
Perhaps there, in Morois, where the fires burn all summer?
There, in the Fosse Commune, the fever bog? If they had not tried
to trick us—if a child hadn't mimicked our cupped hands—

we reared back on our destriers and left those mud-daubed cabins
wreathed in flames—lance to the banked coals,
thrust to the wattle—and rode on in silence
in the chill of evening with the smell of smoke
growing a little stronger at each trick of the wind
and every path we chose was one they had suggested.

2
That mighty adventure eluded us.

I could not tell you what it is: a cup, a dish, a trophy,
Joseph of Arimathea's chipped vessel: a mystery to give us
the power over ourselves that we have over others.

———————

All we had to show the Queen was wounds: Borhold
his mangled thumb, Bors his sutured belly,
Palafox his missing eyelid.

My wound displayed no scab, no blemish.
No flailing axe made it, no pot of lit oil.
Yet it was me she chose. *Tristan, show me your wound.*

Assignations

1
I trembled before each meeting, and trembled after.

Hidden outside her tower, I charmed Iseult with birdsong.
Thrush ecstatic but with a questioning hiccup,
obsessive wheedling finch, indifferent wren,
heartbroken nightingale, ironic cuckoo.

She never answered. Brangien fetched me at midnight.

2
I stepped into the Queen's gray eyes and crossed the horizon.
During the dry-mouth moment together, I spoke in platitudes
of Avalon, Island of Immortality, how all our grief
will have no body to house it, and batter against those shores,
but those cliffs are granite and there are paths
only the goats know, and the fisher-martens, and the newly dead.
I told her of Ysinvitrain, further north, the Glass Kingdom,
where all things are transparent, bread and the knife to cut it,
even the invisible wound, even a lover's mind, and the eye itself.
I realized I was babbling about death, like a child
who found a feather, and I forced myself to compliment her
on her hair knot, her obsidian clasp. She was so vivid
I could not look at her directly, even when I was on top of her.
It was like praising a fire. She stopped listening.
When I caught my breath—always during the meetings my breath
surged against me—she prodded me with questions:
where could a boat land under those screes? Then the encounter
was over. We had slept together. Or not. I said goodbye
as you might take leave of night itself. In the third watch
I was almost happy to be me, just another sword, paid off
with a title, allowed to doze armed cap-à-pie in the royal chamber
among the alaunts' hot mouths, and dream of the King's bed.

3
Alone, I could almost see and touch her, when we made love
she was faes, the caul of the Absolute hid her naked body.

The King's Chamber

Tristan

A gazehound, dozing with eyes open,
stared at me with a profound knowing ignorance.
His nostrils flared, inhaling my lineage
and venal sin, without interrupting his dream.

I crept into the bedroom and lay among the dogs:
Castillian alaunts with ears trimmed to points,
who sleep in armor, dim-witted mastiffs, so imitative
they might nip a spurred horse, terriers
trembling to flush out imaginary enemies.

Each snored according to his breed.
Elkhounds snoozed on top of otterhounds.
Beagles hunted in obsessive unreal circles.
Greyhounds rippled with trance sprints. So dogs too
have a voice that tells them not to act in dreams.

My own mutt curled up at a distance, ashamed to know me.

The kennets and harriers twitched and writhed,
from their thick faint furious cries I deduced
a wounded rabbit, a feist in heat, an adored master,
as Apollonius says we surmise a world from the evidence
of our uncontrollable senses. Sometimes a sleeper drooled
on my cheek, or pinned my wrist with a paw,
or enclosed my ankle with a soft in-bite
exactly like the pang of my own dreams.

Once I drowsed and woke with a scabrous tongue
curling in my mouth. A bloodhound glanced at me
with lugubrious cloudy eyes, and when I started,
rolled to the wall with an absent moan.

So loudly they slept in a vortex of breath
on the straw bed, among bones gnawed to shards,

while snow tumbled like dice in a high slit window
and two guards slept upright, leaning on spears.

Out of that roar of panting and muffled cries
I heard Iseult's breath, a thread I followed
all the way back to childhood, to the first night
when my mother died birthing me in the birch forest.

Then I crawled onto that high golden bed
and snuggled between the monarchs. He murmured thickly,
darling, I answered in a thin voice, darling.

I turned to my Queen and in that darkness
we thought to enter the pupil of God's eye
before he created us, when he was surprised
the light he made to end his loneliness was good.

We loved each other as we are commanded to, politely,
efficiently, with the King's dreaming arm covering us,
until the cock crowed at false dawn
and a faint bell tolled matins.

I whispered goodbye and slithered over bunched pugs
who shivered with a milder, more inward twitch,
beginning to negotiate endings to their dreams,
commencing to know each other and trade soft nips.
Their eyes lit, but not yet with the light of the mind.

I passed like a thought between the spearheads
and vanished down the winding torch-lit corridors.
I reached my chamber, bolted the door,
congratulated myself and stumbled

because I was walking in blood. That secret joy
had reopened my wound and a trail led back
from my cold bed to the King's embrace.

The trumpet sounded fortissimo *wake, wake,*
about to crack in the cold.

———————

The Horse

So we galloped towards Morois.

Or rather, I galloped, Tristan spurred.
Ahead of us the forest lay and soon towered
—there is no path to enter, you enter
by choice after forced choice, until
it hurts like fate: duck, swerve and squeeze
between almost-clearing and almost-thicket
constrained by the rhythm of gaps between trunks,
zones of ignorance between those lordly names

PINE   CEDAR   OAK   ROWAN   YEW   SYCAMORE   BIRCH.

The play of light and shadow intensified
and we were inside, as if inside the mind,
where you can only be in one thought, infinitely far
from all other thoughts, and all thoughts are equal.

He thought of her, she thought of winter.
Or so I surmise. Her hand held the reins
with such subtlety I could have been ruled
by God's will or the night wind.

So we entered Morois. Had it been Brocéliande,
Forest of Enchantment, or Le Mans, Forest of Majesty,
or even Gorre, Forest of the Dead, someone might have thought
to curry me, find me brackish water, perhaps comb
the chafing burrs from my hopelessly tangled mane.

But this was Morois, Forest of Love, and I just stumbled
forward, and forward again, as if there were no past
or future, waiting for that prick in my salty flank.

Everyone in This Story Speaks Except Me   *Iseult*

Even the words. The chords. The silence. I can only think.

I miss my father's Galway house, the crisp bed I made myself.
Call me ruthless but these days whirl forward.
I am Queen of the Land of No Sleep. Why do they give me power?

I love him for no reason, as you might laugh at the pine breeze.
But he will test every gesture in Morois.

Once we could make each other strange as dawn just by undoing
one button, always the same button. Now we run to the shadows.

Once Satan appeared to Saint Marie d'Oignies and whispered,
this world is a dream. She answered, *can't you hear the leper's*
                                         bell?

Now the first pines rise out of the cornrows, the elm crest
looms suddenly, we come to the threshold, the last hedgerow.

The horse rolls his red-veined eye. How Tristan must spur.
The Absolute drives him. The charm of wholeness.
But God is a broken man. A person and the loss of a person.

Yew branches draw back like bows. An opening will find us.
Now to learn what a servant knows. Cold and hunger.

How not to eat or sleep. How not to have a child.

The Living Spring

In my breathing shadow
the lovers hear their voices
confused with mine,
promising a slate roof,
a gate, a child, respite
from the Absolute.
Let them sleep.

Doesn't God love them
because they are like him,
too broken to obey
the rules of death?

In my ambit
birdsong is slurred,
nightingale's loneliness,
famished thrush, sparrow
pining in the cold,
each charged
with rapt indifference.

Rest while I tremble.
Isn't God himself
stubborn as water?

Ceol Sidhe

Tristan

She cut herself a harp from green rowan
that only the faes may cull.

She stood in the scrim of ash leaves
wielding my sword without permission.

I thought we would negotiate
in the wild, she would be less a Queen.
But no. Each day she wears her robe and crown
more imperiously, though they are pollen and dew.

Who am I, not even an audience, a gawker,
bystander at the heart of my own Adventure?

The strings she spindled from mulberry root,
guts of a snared vole, and the Master,
Re, from her cloth-of-gold sleeve.

The pegs were willow, the waist and belly ash.

Without being asked, she scoured my sword
with horse-tail ferns and creek-bottom sand,
and left that Damascene blade sharper.

All dusk I watched her tune, testing each note
against a pitch that does not exist.
Then she began the labor of undoing, tempering
each Absolute before it imposed a system.

At last the strings moved like living rain.
Was she listening in those austere chords
for a command, a secret message? From whom?

She held her wrist cocked, motionless, while her thumbs
inscribed circles, like a wasp groping for a scent,
after the style of the Morne Mountain masters.

Her silence deepened, clarified, and became harmony.

She played heedlessly, flawlessly, like a woman waking
after long sleep, or settling to meat after famine.

She sang thinly, in a language I can't understand,
Alaric, Mogrian, or High Welsh. Once I heard my name
and thrilled to its strangeness on those half-parted lips.
But she turned away from me, away from the fire,
towards the glade where the eye of an animal
or basilisk or lost soul gleamed like a pinhole.

Then I heard Mark, the name Logres, and her voice
modulated in dirge rhythm to the extreme past
as if that were a thirteenth key. All night I watched
as the shadows the flame cast, flame-colored themselves,
bowed to her, because she was Queen, or because she was keening.

Surely if she loved me, the key would be ecstasy—
to be alone together, secluded in a forest?

She was like God, she didn't want intimacy,
just to be right, always right, like the wind and rain.

Once or twice she lost her place and counted a few bars
in my language, but backwards, to the correct measure.

At dawn she cleared her throat and wrapped the harp
in a cinquefoil wimple I'd given her and huddled
naked under jute in straw. I knelt beside her
until my knees ached, listening to her breath
in case I might interpret a catch.

She smelled of deer tallow with which she greased
her shanks against the cold, and crushed basil.

I thought I heard the exile harp answer her
from the direction of Brocéliande, modulating carefully,
like a spider descending a thread, minor to diminished.

At last the sun rose, light tightened like a bass string
in withered alder branches, then slackened. It was day.
The finches sang freely, in pairs, each to each,
and there too I heard my name, forwards and backwards,
and hers, the King's, and the hour of our death.

The Self

When
we
rolled
in mottled
oak leaves
I
shone,
though
the high
hawk
saw
just
two
naked
fugitives.

The Other World

3

With every second thought, Tristan builds
the other world, out of moth quiver,
dangling webs, shudder-path of a dragonfly
suspended a blink in shafts of evening—
from cumulus shadow and impending rain
his axe-mind hacks Yes and No—
he can't stand her reproof, can't bear her smile.
He adores her but shouldn't, she doesn't love him
but must, summer but winter, red-eyed monster
or pure knight, he is Tantris, his wound throbs—

2

that other world is Ysinvitrain,
Glass Island, where the eye can see itself,
a lover's will is transparent, that twig bed
is softer than this, those great oaks
soak up calcium and sap, these pines
wither. There love is action,
here it is a sigh.

1

Tomorrow the King will find the fugitives
as they doze exhausted in a piney neck
and spare them, leaving his sword
to shine between their bodies.
Fortune will reverse.

The Dog

The horse Beau Joueur, who should be called Gros Joueur,
keeps me awake all night rubbing his rump against smooth beech.
He snorts, deliberately loud. He has nothing to do
except chomp delicious melick: talk about a forest of love!

I followed my masters here because they are helpless
like God or a poor man in the wind and rain.
I tore my coat. Who notices? Who pets me?
They sniff each other like poodles, but with more drama.

If they scold, it is each other, if they wander off
it is from each other, if they train anyone to fetch,
sit, roll over, it is the Other, the undying love.
What hell it must be to hunt on such a tangled leash.

Me they praise absently. *Good Dog!* The Other
has a thousand faults which they tally in secret
until a tirade overflows: *you Always . . . you Never . . .*

Inwardly they denounce each other, but to whom?
The trees can't understand them. Neither can the music,
too high-pitched for their hearing. The birds don't care.

Because they are lovers, each second they share
is eternity, fate drives them forward,
they have no clue how to scamper, how to prance.

Sex baffles them. Victory or defeat? Why always more so?
Fucking makes their bodies a thorny thicket.
She flinches at his wound. He cries for her loneliness.

Perhaps through the scrim of desire they may glimpse
the actual forest: alder leaves like wringing hands,
a nuthatch marching straight up a tall cedar.

These woods are full of deer, boar, elk, and bear,
but the lovers' longing is a magic cloak
that makes all other creatures invisible.

I have to guard them from wind, rain, and their minds.
They fascinate me, like the small dead things in the sedge.

Tristan losing footing, manacled by his arguments.
Iseult who misses salt, bells, and his absence.

All night they moan, or choose not to, the horse farts,
and I have no Other except a touch of gray along my muzzle
I can glimpse by squinting: maybe I too am dying of love?

Her Decision

1

Her mind is like the elm, shag-barked and vase-cresting.
Her consent is like mossy ground, secreting dangerous give.

Her will is a swiftly advancing radiant cloud,
always the same but different, trailing deep shadow.

2

Once knights hammered each other to pig-iron
for one crook of her little finger.

Now Iseult shivers beside me, her bitter resolve
hops like a sparrow in frost-tinged sedge.

Her decisions are irrevocable. She doesn't know she made them.
I must make her confess she found my flaw. She'll leave me.

Easier to convince nightfall and the violent elm leaves
whirling on a fixed point that exists nowhere.

3

When I lie on top, or under her, my mind clears
and I can analyze our situation. Winter coming,

acorn bread, twig bed, even the dog growing sullen.
All other times, my brain swarms with Absolutes.

4

We troubadour-knights are the first to practice *fin amor*.
Our fathers were brutes, our grandfathers dripping spears.

I believe in the donnai, the assag, but within reason.
Let her control me, but just for a harp cadence.

But we are stranded in eternity, in Morois. Here God
moves in the pines like a breeze that knows what it is.

An Opening

I searched for the hollow where we once lay.
It seemed the timothy tips were still bent,
the sedge sticky, the ants jittery.

I came to a circle of split stones.
I knew it for the old fire and collected peat moss,
antler velvet and birch bark, and struck flint
but the flame that rose gave no heat.
I could put my hand in it and watch the nail blacken
and begin to curl inward, and still feel nothing.
And I had thought madness was suffering.
Time did not pass. The coals flinched, the sparks
launched themselves like soundless bees.
There was no connection between char and ash.
Dawn was a paler, more begrudging midnight.
I couldn't tell the sun from the hole it made in heaven.
I couldn't feel God's grace though it burnt a hole in me.

Sometimes in my madness I tried to love myself
but my hand grew tired, and felt betrayed.
My sex was like her: adamant, too smooth.

I tried to strike myself with my sword
just to have a grievance to occupy my empty mind.
I heard it whistle toward me and resigned myself
to hell, since this was mortal sin. But no.
The blade sundered my stunned shadow.
I stood apart, watching, profoundly watching,
as if the world had become a picture of itself.

I dreamt Iseult would love me, and she did.
I had to test it, as if it happened in sleep.

Like any servant, wind and rain broke me.
I dreamed I would go mad, and I am.

I dreamed I would become you, the listener,
and find a clearing in the forest.

The Grail

I am a smashed robin's egg,
a hollow acorn the beetle drilled,
a cup with a hairline crack
that holds the world to come.

Another Iseult, who didn't know my faults, might be easier—
a demure girl I didn't love so much, and there were many
in that foggy neatly tilled country I escaped to: Iseult
of the White Hands, Iseult of the Red Lips, Iseult
of the Flaxen Hair. I married the first who said yes,
though in bed I felt just the throbbing of my wound.

Other Tristans crowded the taverns—perhaps the harp
had made our names common as our destiny:
Tristan the Better Lover, Tristan the Less Mad.
I tried to avoid them: one less petulant quarrel
over who killed a vole or rabbit. I made a living
hunting small monsters, no bigger than a crayfish
or prawn, and giving private fencing lessons.

Time closed like a book. My wound stung less,
a diminishing music. I who once pretended
to be mad, and went mad, now disguised myself
with white whiskers. I became reasonable, remote:
maybe things will work out, maybe the world will end,
I thought. I enjoyed the local cuisine: bisque,
ratatouille, and a chalk-white plummy Vouvray.
I savored a village renown, and the jealousy
of ancient cankered harpers. My body began to fail.

Sickness marked me with its waxy pencil
and called me in its coy voice, by my opposite name:
"Come here, Tantris." At once my days shortened
towards that winter whose wind I shall not feel.
The tip of the yew leaf curled inward.

Then I had a caravelle fitted out, with ash oars,
a damask bed, and red sails so I would not live
in case of *No.*

I sent it to Logres with my last silver coin,
certain she would come, certain it would be too late.

Queen of the Land of No Sleep

1

I didn't hesitate. I adore him. But what were my choices?
Deny the Adventure or die of plague with a Tristan
fussed over by a mild wife with mushroom-white hands?
I hear him argue: *everyone who dies dies of love.*
Suffering gives him that right?

So be it, little mad knight whose madness cooled
in a colder bed. No more ziphius, no more ichnumeon.
Iseult is still your monster.

Every great love has an obstacle. Ours was us.
The Law was carved in us like a child's name in a tree.

2

The Chronicle tells the rest fairly accurately.
I packed nothing and rode to the port at dawn
with many a backward glance at Brangien,
who didn't wave, knowing I would never return.
I found Tristan's ship behind a stand of willows
whose roots must have been immune to salt,
growing right down to the ocean. I remanded the horse
in excellent custody. I hailed the captain
who scooped up his dice lazily and greeted me
with a shrug. Tristan's charm was wearing off the world.

The end you know. How the storm battered us.
The purser wanted to throw me overboard for Syax
but the cabin boy argued I was faes. I was used to that.

Then the calm came. That sea was not just transparent
but seemed to magnify my gaze. Pearls glinted
on the close sea-floor. The water shone thinner
than in a human ocean. The oar had no purchase
and flailed through that radiance.

The delay-fish had latched onto our rudder
and no oar or punting-pole could dislodge it.

How the crew missed their wives and lovers!
To catch the faintest breath of twilight
they piled on sail after sail. They hoisted
Tristan's satin bed sheets, then the red sail
whose import will kill him,

and I did not command them not to
and cannot say why not.

The Adventure of Tristan and Iseult

I am growing old. I am starting to fade.
I am increasingly tongue-tied.
With great pains and blandishments
the harpist coaxes me to the Re string.

There I last only a few measures—
spasm on silk sheets, come in a forest,
mad eye of a dying monster, sizzling
like yolk on a griddle. Then diminuendo.

The text is filling with lacunae:
[. . .] ash leaf with an erratic vein [. . .]
[. . .] red nubbin on a spruce twig [. . .]
[. . .] basswood in a halo of bees [. . .]

The chronicler pauses, his mind full of twilight.
He chooses fresh pumice and abrades the vellum—
caul of a stillborn calf—and starts to doodle
in the soft margin.
                    Tristan will stop muttering
and learn to live in hours instead of eternity.
Iseult will apologize, form alliances, rule.

They tell lies. They come to know themselves
despite the philtre, the pines, and the King's fury,
out of habit and grievance. They too fade.

That love endures, cold as the wind and rain.

1

They burnt my harp. They said it was faes.
They cut the strings and called me
a chronicler of heretic adulterers.

2

Such a rage to pose questions.
Why does God permit sin?
Why does he pardon traitors?

Why did he allow his own son to die?
Why can't he return to the past
and deflect the lance from that naked flank—
why must he move forward, always forward?
What drives him?

Under the thumbscrew
my responses were random, perhaps just grunts—
maybe they trusted them
because they were given by suffering, not a person,
as if a broken jug could talk, or a useless inch of string—
they nodded to themselves.

Clearly they had lived a long time
with just questions and answers
and the slow mounting cry
was a better possibility. They inscribed it
in a fat book—no doubt all vowels—
which made it part of history:

a complicated game between good and evil,
memorized by children, carved in the plinth
of marble statues, not something that actually happens
to a thumb, a tiny part of the body,
less than a thousandth of its weight,

nothing that could dare to call itself I
or be commemorated, though it breaks
like a man, a kingdom, a belief.

A Night in Brooklyn

Waking in Greenpoint in Late August

We wanted so much that there be a world
as we lay naked on our gray-striped mattress,
staring up at a trowel mark on the eggshell-blue ceiling
and waiting, waiting for twilight, darkness, dawn,
marriage, the child, the hoarse names of the city—
let there be a universe in which these lovers can wash
at the pearling spigot, and lick each other dry.

Making Shelves

In that lit window in Bushwick
halfway through the hardest winter
I cut plexiglass on a table saw,
coaxing the chalked taped pane
into the absence of the blade,
working to such fine tolerance
the kerf abolished the soft-lead line.
I felt your eyes play over me
but did not turn—dead people
were not allowed in those huge factories.
I bargained: when the bell rang
I would drink with you on Throop
under the El, quick pint of Night Train
but you said *no*. Blood jumped

from my little finger, power
snapped off, voices summoned me
by name, but I waved them back
and knelt to rule the next line.

Red Antares in a Blue Mirror

On that close-nap futon
she taught me the difference
between being and becoming,
when she had finished
it was still twilight, a cricket
singing I, I, not furiously,
but with a cool insistence,
and I understood how the universe
was created—how it fit in a pinhead
fourteen billion years ago
when the first second lasted
almost forever, then it flew
in a trillion pieces and now
it obeys laws we recognize
the way a pet comes to look
like its owner: she was washing
at the cold tap, she was binding
back her copper hair, but I
had been given those absolute weapons:
suffering, abnegation, miracle:
and I had to use them
if only by counting, counting
until it was night and the rain
simmered in the dog's huge eyes.

The Dead Remember Brooklyn

It is the great arguments
we are proud of, over a nibbled peach,
hair in the comb, a faulty lube job;
the reconciliations were always breathless
in borrowed rooms, sometimes in Queens
or Staten Island, we touched each other
shyly—we reminded each other
of loneliness and funk and beautiful pigeons
with oil-slick necks, cooing bitterly—
but there we lost each other,
in forgiveness; keeping score,
being wounded even in triumph,
walking home down leafy avenues
etched with the faint double line
of extinct trolleys, caressing
carved hearts under a sheen of sap
with a ragged nail, sleeping alone,
choosing the dream of betrayal,
entering by the wide door
and waking dead—there
we were superb. In Brooklyn
we held our own.

The Bars

After work I'd go to the little bars
along the bright green river, Chloe's Lounge,
Cloverleaf, Barleycorn, it was like dying
to sit at 5:00 p.m. with a Bud so cold
it had no taste, it stung my hand,
when I returned home I missed my keys
and rang until my wife's delicate head
emerged in her high window and retreated
like a snail tucked into a luminous shell—
I couldn't find my wallet, or my paycheck,
though I drank nothing, only a few sips
that tasted like night air, a ginger ale,
nevertheless a dozen years passed, a century,
always I teetered on that high stool
while the Schlitz globe revolved so slowly,
disclosing Africa, Asia, Antarctica,
unfathomable oceans, radiant poles,
until I was a child, they would not serve me,
they handed me a red hissing balloon
but for spite I let it go, for the joy
of watching it climb past Newton Tool & Die
for fear of cherishing it, for the pang
of watching it vanish and knowing myself
both cause and consequence.

Sonny Stitt at the Blue Coronet

His fingers don't seem to move
as he rips through secondary dominants
of *Boplicity, Simone, Ray's Idea.*
The alto is a golden fishhook.

Why such blazing tempi when he'll die
in six weeks? Perhaps in heroin
there's a calm in which you can fit
a thousand notes into one beat.

Drums, bass, Hammond organ—
these are unnamed men, faces
you've met all your life
and bargained with, nodded to,
yet they have no difficulty
with the subtlest modulation.

The audience is three drunks,
one cursing an imaginary waitress,
one mumbling apologies, one sleeping.

Now try to eat your extremely salted cashews
so slowly there will always be one left.

The North Side

I took a job at the Arnold Grill,
topping off drafts with a paddle
for the Saint Johnsbury truckers.

Tuesday nights my father came in
to buy a shot of muscatel
and nurse it in a far booth
beside a small jukebox
which he plied with quarters.

He was dead so the smoke
and obscenities did not bother him.

At 3:00 a.m. I began tallying my tips—
a fortune in Canadian pennies.

Once, I confronted him:
why do you keep coming?
Can't you rest? And why Tuesday?

He was hurt. He averted his fine eyes
and joined a conversation
about Billy Martin—

had he ruined Vida Blue?
A waitress laughed—apparently
my father knew nothing of the forkball—
and next Tuesday he did not come.

No one missed him.
The pool players cleaned the table,
rack after rack, adjusting the score
with beads on a string in midair,

the dart players paused, with pursed lips,
pushing the feathers through air
as if they had just found an opening,

but my father had not returned,
not even as a ghost, not even
as a tremor in a bettor's hand.

I locked the iron door at first light,
lowered the steel shutters,
clicked the seven padlocks,
and instead of my father,
to whom I'd spoken all my life
with bitterness, with sarcasm,

I spoke to that uncertain moment
between false dawn and dawn
when the traffic roars north,
just streaks of trapped light,
lamps go out in the charity ward,
and the tenements light up,
the highest floors first:

Why can't you rest, I said.

Letter from Home

1

She writes: we would have voted against the war
but all the candidates opposed it.

We joined a march in dead of winter.
Weekend clerks gathered to applaud,
clapping to warm their numb hands.
In the tenements, hand-lettered signs supported us.

The soldiers said, *we will not fight,*
and the generals, *there is no cause.*
Whom would we invade? she writes:
we were the greatest power, perhaps of all time.
Then the war began in the corner of the eye.
At first it was mild and demanded nothing.
Now to want to die would be a privilege.
Now the invasion writes these words and can't stop.

2

They practice torture here, she says,
in the hospital, in the maze of corridors
color-coordinated for the insides of the body.
The laws allow it, but only as a last resort.
Only if the city might be destroyed otherwise.

3

We've created an external mind, she writes.
It has made our world small as a withheld breath.
If you want a weapon you have only to imagine it.

4

Still a window blazes all night.
Still the cars pass.

The Trapper Keeper

The child lost the essay she wrote
on rainfall in state capitals—
Pierre, Bismarck, Olympia—
left it on the Corona bus
and she was inconsolable
as if she forgot twilight itself.
So I set out for the Depot
past the tavern and bodega,
stockyard and shunting yard, there
where drivers relax on raffia seats
reading the gospels in Coptic or Aramaic,
and I found it: her intricate binder
green with stickers of frogs.
I slogged through triplicate forms
and lugged her homework home.
She and I were lost in fortune,
she couldn't believe her luck
or I my power, the Methodist sirens
whined very faintly, she stayed up late
writing about rainfall in Willamette,
Boise, Havre de Grace, Sioux Falls.
But I couldn't sleep for happiness,
half-wishing that dog-eared folder
had stayed safe in loss,
in the past where our steel door
with its buckling tin number
is locked like all the other tenements.

The Living Will

I rode the subway to Gilead
where my mother lay in a coma.

When we passed aboveground
I saw children playing ball
on a little diamond
in a haze of dust—

a cheerleader whirled upside down,
a bald coach placed a zero
in a grooved slot.

A home run soared into dusk
and the children froze,
but one walked away in tears.

He was talking to himself.
I tried to read his lips.

Then we entered Flatbush:
padlocked furniture stores:
in one window, a fringed lamp blazed,
in the next, an immense sofa
like a god's knees—signs
read *Sale! Sale!* but on the streets
there was no one.

At the border of Bensonhurst
a nun dragged a balky collie
on a retractable leash.

An old man in rubber sandals
lugged a sign *Repent* and argued
with the air beside him.

At Bath Beach a gap-toothed kid
waved to me from a marble stoop
and I was no longer a witness,
no longer a passerby.

I patted my pockets
for the wadded form
with the strange stiff language
that means *no life support.*

Freedom and Chance

She says, there is another city, exactly like this:
same sardonic cat, complacent dog, fat-chested sparrow
trilling its brains out before daybreak, identical abandon
and thrilling sorrow, familiar machinery chuffing
in darkness—belt sander, leaf blower, radial arm saw.
But that world is Ditmas Park, this is Dyker Heights.
The law is like wind. It has no self.
There Frank Viola stars, here Julio Franco.
Here light is a wave, there a particle.
Here we marry and play cribbage in a tiny house
with a porch swing and complicated locks.
There, you plod through deserted chain stores
in search of someone you cannot know. Here
the names of God, blurted from passing cars.
There, the milk truck and its loud crate of empties.

A Night in Brooklyn

We undid a button,
turned out the light,
and in that narrow bed
we built the great city—
watertowers, cisterns,
hot asphalt roofs, parks,
septic tanks, arterial roads,
Canarsie, the intricate channels,
the seacoast, underwater mountains,
bluffs, islands, the next continent,
using only the palms of our hands
and the tips of our tongues, next
we made darkness itself, by then
it was time for daybreak
and we closed our eyes
until the sun rose
and we had to take it all to pieces
for there could be only one Brooklyn.

The Present

We made models: this is a moment of happiness,
this is a maple-shaded street, its yellow median line
littered with double wings: someday we might know such things
in our real lives, not just in desire.

We invented Cherryfield, Maine, nine pearl-gray Capes
with sagging porches held together by coats of gesso.
Behind the scrim of birches the Middle Branch River
glittered like the galvanized roof to a tackle shed.

We were quick and replicated a shack with a chalk sign
CHUBBS SMELTS CROAKERS; there was barely time to read it
before it whirled into the past. And she who was driving said,
we know the coming disaster intimately but the present is
                                        unknowable.

Which disaster, I wondered, sexual or geological? But I was shy:
her beauty was like a language she didn't speak and had never
                                   heard.

Then we were in Holyfield and it was the hour when the child
waves from a Welcome mat, his eyes full of longing, before turning
inward to his enforced sleep. We waved back but we were gone.

The hour when two moths bump together above a pail of lures.

The hour when the Coleman lamp flickers in the screen house
above the blur of cards being shuffled and dealt amazingly fast.

All my life I have been dying, of hope and self-pity,
and an unknown force has been knitting me back together.
It happens in secret. I want to touch her and I touch her
and it registers on the glittering gauges that make the car darker
and swifter and we come to the mountains and this is all I ever
                                   wanted:

to enter the moth's pinhead eye, now, and never return.

Damariscotta

1

How we loved to create a world.

Out of *gray* we made the pin-oak leaves
with their saw teeth and odd waxy sheen,
dry and matte to the touch, out of *granite*
we made the marriage house, and always
we added a flaw which we called *fire*
or *time* or *the stranger.*

2

A drop of water on the lip of a jug,
trembling, trying to hold on
for another second to the idea of sphericity—
that was us, our nakedness.

3

We worked to thwart our happiness
because it was so unexpected;
suffering tasted like our mouths.

4

We had a flagstone path, a pond, four birches,
a dog racing in tight circles, helpless
against the dream of fresh snow.

Tomorrow that red Schwinn with training wheels
must find a way to pedal itself.

5

World like a child who learned to walk
beyond our outstretched hands.

The Simulacra

They were driving into the mountains, helplessly married,
sometimes touching each other's cheek with a fingernail
gingerly: the radio played ecstatic static: certain roads
marked with blue enamel numbers led to cloud banks,
or basalt screes, or dim hotels with padlocked verandas.
Sometimes they quarreled, sometimes they grew old,
the wind was constant in their eyes, it was their own breeze,
they made it. Small towns flew past, Rodez, Cahors,
limestone quarries, pear orchards, children racing
after hoops, wobbling when their shadows wavered,
infants crying for fine rain, old women on stoops
darning gray veils—and who were we, watching?
Doubles, ghosts, the ones who would tell of the field
where they pulled over, bluish tinge of the elms, steepness
of the other's eyes, glowworm hidden in its glint,
how the rain was dusk and now is darkness.

Andalusian *Coplas* & Song Fragments
Versions of anonymous originals

1
To play my guitar
for the dark girl
I washed my hands with mint.

2
To forget you
I'd need another sun,
another moon, commandments
from another God.

3
Go ask your mother
to put you in an alcove
and light candles in front of you.
Tell her I'm done with you.

4
Run and tell your mom
to shear and fleece you—
let her give you suck again
and teach you to be a man.

5
Because I'm a stranger
I ask the locals,
who is that dark girl
who looks so good in mourning?

6
That idiot girl thought I'd cry.
Doesn't she know the taverns
sell little portions of happiness?

7
I knocked three times
at midnight on your iron gate.
For someone dying of love, little girl,
you're a heavy sleeper.

8
Your eyes and mine tangled
like blackberry vines
under the owner's fence.

9
A poor man stinks of death.
Throw him in the pit.
Jingle in your pocket?
Requiescat in pace. Amen.

Five Spanish Riddles
Versions of anonymous originals

1
I'm a terrible guest,
nobody wants me,
but you can't remember me
unless you entertain me—
who am I?
Hunger.

2
Green, all green,
green birth, and now
I sit on top of God?
The crown of thorns.

3
What did the shepherd
see in the mountains
that the King can't see,
the Pope on his throne won't see,
God Almighty shall never see?
His equal.

4
I walked down a road that didn't come back
and they took off the cape that I never wore.
I went to a lettuce patch and picked apples.
The owner of the chestnuts arrived.
—What are you doing in my lettuce patch?
—I'm gathering acorns
sweet as artichoke honey.
What am I?
A lame riddle.

5
Five oxen plowing
with a single harrow—
what dark work is this
in a fallow field?
The hand writing.

A Night in Cáceres

We gave each other the absolute gift.
And we were scared.
We wanted to take it back.
We didn't know how to mention it:
we hardly knew our own names.
Give me that night back.
That fly fumbling in the webs.
That touch, like moonlight on your arm,
but free, not determined by the laws
of distance and falling bodies.
A thrush chirring after midnight
with great confidence and brokenness.
The hush of the Tajo River
as it pools towards Navas.
We listened for the other's breath.
Sometimes we heard it, sometimes rain.
We slept in the crook of the arm.
At first light we flinched.
There was no other. No such gift.
In the mirror, just a high cloud
and Venus, brighter in daylight.

There Is No Time, *She Writes*

We have to bomb the rebel cities
from a great height, find shelter
for the refugees, carry a sick kitten
to the shade of a blighted elm,
fall in love, walk by the breakwater,
learn the words to separate,
marry, see a lawyer, negotiate,

and always the wind seethes
in the blade-like leaves,
always the ant under its burden,
proud and indomitable, *she writes,*
always the faint music, the touch
of the other's hand, and no way
to return, or even turn,
no way to see ourselves:

writing this, I pressed so hard
she says, the words are embedded
in the grain of the desk
and it is dark but I sense you
listening, trying to frame an answer
there where the dark turns inward
and a small bell chimes
in the stupefying heat.

The Power Point

That century passed in spurts. All our responses—rage, shame—
were etched on our foreheads with a steel-nib Bic.
Yet we could not feel them. Barely remember their names.
Between the plenary and keynote we aged a dozen years.
During the breakout sessions we gained back a few breaths,
a moment of regained clarity when we spoke of Kara melting
and allowed ourselves to choke with passion. Passion
we could not feel. That hall swam with soft glints
reflected off watch crystals, iPhones, chandeliers,
racing screens that cannot move. Always the PowerPoint
advanced from whale to dolphin to pollack to krill.
The image clicked forward like days, frame to frame,
though we longed to know what happens in between.
The voice followed sinuously. It cannot stop.
How we missed the blue chalk dust of our apprenticeship,
our yellow dog-eared legal pads crawling with statistics
inscribed by hand, poison in Jacmel, Bhopal, Battambang.
The numbers themselves had grown bland, oddly distanced
from the marlite on which they were projected.
Yet we were children a second ago, eager to learn
to inscribe the great zero, our mouths open,
teaching ourselves to spell, tell time, and tie our shoes,
sailor knot, scout knot, as if your love could stop us
drawing those knots tighter and tighter in the mind.

Psalm to Be Read with Closed Eyes

Ignorance will carry me through the last days,
the blistering cities, over briny rivers
swarming with jellyfish, as once my father
carried me from the car up the narrow steps
to the white bed, and if I woke, I never knew it.

Acknowledgments

The chronology of this collection reflects the order in which the books were written, not necessarily the order in which they were published. I'd like to acknowledge and thank the editors and journals where many poems in the volume were first seen over the years, including these below, where the "new" pieces in this book first appeared:

The American Poetry Review: "The Screen," "The Fire," "Not Yet America."

Barrow Street: "Marriage in the Mountains."

Field: "The Commands," "A Country of Strangers."

Hanging Loose: "Money."

Harvard Review: "The Unendurable Tests."

The Manhattan Review: "In the City of Statues," "In the Winter of Painted Swastikas" (published as "Days of 2017").

The New Yorker: "The Body," "A Clearing on Ruth Island."

The Paris Review: "Caligula."

Plume: "The Detentions," "Game with a Mad Bounce."

Poetry: "The Chime."

Poetry Ireland: "This Life."

The Poetry Review (UK): "Early Morning, Late Summer, Unmade Bed."

poets.org: "Showers" (also published in *Le Journal des Pòetes,* Brussels, Belgium).

Resistance, Rebellion, Life, Knopf: "Marbles and a Dead Bee."

The Times Literary Supplement (UK): "Flora of the Boreal Forest" (also in *Recours au Poeme,* Paris, France), "Ischia" (first published as "Ventimiglia"), "Evening in the Pines," "A Lullaby."

Together in a Sudden Strangeness, Knopf: "Order to Disperse," "Conversation Behind the White Curtain" (also in *Coming out of Isolation,* Kistrech, Nairobi, Kenya).

Upstreet: "The White Prisons" (also in *I Can't Breathe,* Kistrech, Nairobi, Kenya).

The Yale Review: "The Arrow Creek Fire."

Special thanks to my editor, Deborah Garrison, who conceived of this project, and to Todd Portnowitz and Josie Kals. My gratitude also to Martha Rhodes, Robert Hershon, and Gerald Freund.

Thanks to MacDowell, the Corporation of Yaddo, the Friday Harbor Laboratories of the University of Washington, Blue Mountain Center, the Virginia Center for the Creative Arts, the National Endowment for the Arts, the New York Foundation for the Arts, the Whiting Foundation, the Guggenheim Foundation, the Tanne Foundation, and the American Academy of Arts and Letters.

I owe a huge debt to everyone who read, critiqued, published, or supported this work since the 1980s. I don't have space to list every name. But this book wouldn't exist without you.

Index of Titles

A Note About the Author

D. Nurkse is the author of eleven previous books of poetry. His many honors include a Literature Award from the American Academy of Arts and Letters and a Guggenheim fellowship. His poems have appeared in periodicals such as *The New Yorker, The American Poetry Review,* and *The Paris Review;* he has taught poetry in prison and, as Brooklyn poet laureate, in local schools and the public library system. He has also worked for human rights organizations. A resident of Brooklyn, he currently teaches in the MFA program at Sarah Lawrence College.

A Note on the Type

This book was set in Fairfield, a typeface designed by the
American artist and engraver Rudolph Ruzicka (1883–1978).

Composed by North Market Street Graphics,
Lancaster, Pennsylvania

Printed and bound by Friesens,
Altona, Manitoba

Design by Michael Collica